RAINER MARIA RILKE

In Translations by M. D. HERTER NORTON
Letters to a Young Poet
Sonnets to Orpheus
Wartime Letters of Rainer Maria Rilke
Translations from the Poetry of Rainer Maria Rilke
The Lay of the Love and Death of Cornet Christopher Rilke
The Notebooks of Malte Laurids Brigge
Stories of God

Translated by STEPHEN SPENDER and J. B. LEISHMAN
Duino Elegies

Translated by JANE BANNARD GREENE and M. D. HERTER NORTON
Letters of Rainer Maria Rilke
Volume One, 1892–1910   Volume Two, 1910–1926

PICASSO: *Les Saltimbanques*

Rainer Maria Rilke

DUINO ELEGIES

THE GERMAN TEXT, WITH AN ENGLISH
TRANSLATION, INTRODUCTION,
AND COMMENTARY BY
J. B. LEISHMAN AND STEPHEN SPENDER

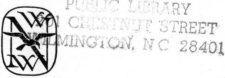
The Norton Library
W · W · NORTON & COMPANY · INC ·
NEW YORK

W. W. Norton & Company, Inc. also publishes *The Norton Anthology of English Literature*, edited by M. H. Abrams et al; *The Norton Anthology of Poety*, edited by Arthur M. Eastman et al; *World Masterpieces*, edited by Maynard Mack et al; *The Norton Reader*, edited by Arthur M. Eastman et al; *The Norton Facsimile of the First Folio of Shakespeare*, prepared by Charlton Hinman; *The Norton Anthology of Modern Poetry*, edited by Richard Ellmann and Robert O'Clair; and the *Norton Critical Editions*.

ISBN 0 393 00155 5

Contents

Preface

IN undertaking this most difficult piece of work, we have tried to devise a method which should achieve, above all, unity of style. Accordingly, J. B. Leishman prepared a draft of the whole work, on the basis of which Stephen Spender prepared a second version; then, with these two versions before him, J. B. Leishman prepared the final version, which was approved by both of us.

For the Introduction and Commentary J. B. Leishman is entirely responsible. He has tried to confine himself to the business of stating facts and attempting elucidations, and, although he has naturally owed much to other scholars, he has owed most of all to Rilke, who still remains the best interpreter of his own works.

Our special thanks are due to Dr. E. L. Stahl and to Herr Paul Obermüller, both of whom read through the manuscript and made many valuable suggestions.

J. B. L.

S. S.

Introduction

I

AFTER the publication of the *Neue Gedichte,* in 1907 and 1908, and of *Malte Laurids Brigge,* in 1910, Rilke, the perpetual beginner, felt that his real task still remained undone.[1] The poem *Wendung (Turning),*[2] written in June, 1914, concludes:

> *Work of sight is achieved,*
> *now for some heart-work*
> *on all those pictures, those prisoned creatures within you!*
> *You conquered them; but do not know them as yet.*
> *Behold, O man within, the maiden within you!—*
> *creature won from a thousand natures, creature*
> *only just won, but never,*
> *as yet, belov'd.*

No longer could he hope

> *from outward forms to win*
> *The passion and the life, whose fountains are within.*

The multitudinous images he had collected must henceforth be regarded as equivalents for inward experiences, as material for 'heart-work,' for the fashioning forth of some ultimate vision of human life and destiny and of the true relationship between the looker and that world on which

[1] For a full account of the restless period of questioning and waiting which followed, see Introduction and Commentary to *Later Poems,* Hogarth Press, 1938.
[2] *Later Poems,* 61.

he had looked so intensely and so long. In 1915, he wrote of the Spanish landscape ("the last I illimitably experienced"): *Everywhere appearance and vision came, as it were, together in the object, in every one of them a whole inner world was exhibited, as though an angel, in whom space was included, were blind and looking into himself. This world, regarded no longer from the human point of view, but as it is within the angel, is perhaps my real task, one, at any rate, in which all my previous attempts would converge.*[3]

A beginning with this 'task' had been made during the winter of 1911–12. In October Rilke visited his friend, Princess Marie von Thurn und Taxis-Hohenlohe, at Schloss Duino, near Trieste, and, from her departure in the middle of December until her return in the following April, he remained in the castle alone. One day he received a troublesome business letter which required an immediate and careful answer; to settle his thoughts, he went out into the roaring wind and paced to and fro along the bastions, the sea raging two hundred feet below. Suddenly he stopped, for it seemed that from the midst of the storm a voice had called to him:

> *Wer, wenn ich schriee, hörte mich denn aus der Engel Ordnungen?*
>
> *Who, if I cried, would hear me among the angelic orders?*

Taking out the note-book he always carried with him, he wrote down these words, together with a few verses which seemed to follow of their own accord. He knew that the god had spoken at last. Quietly returning to his room, he dispatched the troublesome letter; and by the evening of that day the *First Elegy* had been written. He sent a copy of it to Princess Marie on January 21st, and the *Second* was written shortly afterwards. She also reports that he told her that the beginnings of all the other *Elegies* had been written during this winter in Duino, but, except for the *Third, Tenth,* and, possibly, the *Ninth,* her report can hardly be correct.[4]

[3] *Briefe aus den Jahren 1914–1921,* 80.
[4] Marie Thurn und Taxis, *Erinnerungen an Rainer Maria Rilke,* 40–42.

Rilke had to wait ten years before he could complete the task so strangely begun. In January, 1913, he wrote to Lou Andreas-Salomé, from Spain: *Yes, the two Elegies are there,—but I can tell you when we meet how small and how sharply broken a fragment they form of what was then delivered into my power.*[5] The greater part of the *Sixth* and a few lines of the *Ninth Elegies* were written during this visit to Spain: the *Third*, which had been begun at Duino, was completed in Paris during 1913, where, a year later, some small progress was made with the *Sixth* and with a continuation (later rejected) of the first twelve lines of the *Tenth*. Then came the War. How Rilke at first hailed the apparition of the

> *hearsaid, remote, incredible War God*

as a call to intenser living and as an opportunity to learn through suffering; how, for a few days, his heart was beating 'with the beat of the general heart,' and how then, 'ineffably individual as I am,' he shrank away from 'this monstrous universality'; how deeply depressed he was by the vulgarisation of sacrifice and suffering, and how, nevertheless, he still struggled to maintain his double vision, his faith in the ultimate rightness of things, has already been revealed in *Five Songs: August, 1914*, and in the commentary thereon.[6] The bitter *Fourth Elegy* was written at Munich in November, 1915.[7] Looking back, in January, 1920, he wrote: *During almost all the War-years I was . . . waiting in Munich, always thinking it MUST come to an end, not understanding, not understanding, not understanding!* NOT TO UNDERSTAND: *yes, that was my whole occupation during those years—I can assure you, it was not an easy one! For me, the open world was the only possible one, I knew of no other: what did I not owe to Russia,—it has made me all that I am, from there I inwardly set out, all the home of my instinct, all my inward origin is* THERE! *What do I not owe to Paris, and shall never cease to owe her. And to the other countries! I can, could, take nothing*

[5] *Briefe aus den Jahren 1907–1914*, 271.
[6] *Later Poems*, 65.
[7] Cf. *Briefe an seinen Verleger*, 249. The letter is incorrectly assigned to 1915, instead of to 1916.

back,—not for one moment, not in any direction, reject or hate or suspect.[8]

After the Revolution had disappointed his hopes and confirmed his fears, he left Germany in June, 1919, for Switzerland, eager to recover, as he put it, the continuity of his existence, to repair 'the fearful fractures of the year Fourteen,' and to complete the work which had been begun at Duino in 1912. After various unsuccessful attempts to obtain the continuous solitude he needed, he was enabled, through the generosity of a friend, to establish himself, in August, 1921, in the little Château de Muzot (pronounced 'Muzotte'), near Sierre. *I'm now settled,* he wrote, in the following November, *and spinning myself into a primeval tower . . . in the midst of this, beyond all comparison, grand, magnificent landscape.*[9] Utterance and release came to him in February, 1922. On the afternoon of the 9th he was able to telegraph to his Swiss friend, Frau Wunderly-Volkart, *Seven Elegies now generally ready—in any case the most important—Joy and Wonder.* On his way back from the post-office *the Eighth* [presumably the present *Sixth*] *and Ninth finished and formed themselves around smaller and larger earlier fragments.*[10] In the evening he sat down to announce to the friend and publisher who had supported and encouraged and believed in him during so many years that at last, 'after a few days' tremendous obedience of spirit,' he was 'over the hill'; and two days later he wrote to Princess Marie:

At last,
> *Princess,*
at last, the blessed, how blessed day, on which I can announce to you the conclusion—so far as I see—of the
> > *Elegies:*
> > > TEN!

From the last, the great one (with the opening, begun long since in Duino: "Someday, emerging at last from this terrifying vision, may I burst into jubilant praise to responding angels . . .") from this last one, which moreover, even then, was intended to be the last,—from this—

[8] *Briefe aus den Jahren 1914–1921*, 292.
[9] *Briefe aus Muzot*, 40–41.
[10] J. R. von Salis, *Rainer Maria Rilkes Schweizer Jahre*, 95.

my hand is still trembling! Just now, Saturday, the eleventh, at six o'clock in the evening, it's finished!—

All in a few days, there was a nameless storm, a hurricane, in my mind (like that time in Duino), everything in the way of fibre and web in me split,—eating was not to be thought of, God knows who fed me.

But now IT IS. IS,

Amen.

So I've survived up to this, through and through it all. Through it all. And it was this that was needed. ONLY *this.*

One I've dedicated to Kassner. The whole is YOURS, *Princess, how could it fail to be! Will be called:*

THE DUINO ELEGIES

In the book (for I can't give you what has belonged to you from the beginning) I don't intend there to be any dedication, but:

The property of . . . [11]

On the same day he wrote, in very similar phraseology, to Lou Andreas-Salomé, and on the 20th he told her that, 'in a radiant after-storm,' yet another *Elegy,* the present *Fifth,* had been written.[12]

What, exactly, did the 'completion' of the *Elegies* involve? The first four, as we have seen, were already there, and all but the last ten lines of the *Sixth;* the *Fifth, Seventh,* and *Eighth* were written entirely at Muzot, together with all but the first six and the last three lines of the *Ninth,* and all but the first twelve lines of the *Tenth.*[13] And not only were the *Elegies* finished during this tempest of creative activity: between the 2nd and the 20th of February the fifty-five *Sonnets to Orpheus,* which came as a complete surprise, and whose composition preceded and followed that of the *Elegies,* were also written. When, in July, 1922, the Kippenbergs visited Rilke at Muzot, plans were made for a complete edition of his works. He declared that, in every sense of the word,

[11] *Briefe aus Muzot,* 100–1.

[12] This additional *Elegy* did not bring the total number up to eleven; the one which had hitherto stood as the *Fifth* was rejected, and appears in *Later Poems,* 91, as *Antistrophes* (and not, as was there erroneously stated, as *Don't let the fact that it* WAS,—*Childhood, that nameless bond,* 52).

[13] The best summary of the available information on this subject is given by Eudo C. Mason, *Lebenshaltung und Symbolik bei Rainer Maria Rilke,* 211–22.

the edition would be complete. A few poems, a few translations, might still be written, but with the *Elegies* his real work had been concluded: what had been given him to say, he had now said.[14]

In his letters we constantly find him depreciating his own part in these works, speaking of them as having been 'given' to him, and expressing his reverent thankfulness for the 'grace' that enabled him to conceive and complete them. The mere fact of their existence, the long and painful stages on the road to their completion, came to possess for him, as it may also, perhaps, come to possess for us, a kind of symbolic value, as a pledge that ultimately, in spite of all, 'man *shall* find grace.' *That a man who had felt himself, through the disastrous onset of those years, cloven to his foundations, into a Once and a therewith incompatible, dying Now: that such a man should experience the grace of being able to perceive how, in still more secret depths,* BENEATH *this torn-open cleft, the continuity of his work and of his mind was being restored . . . , seems to me more than a merely private occurrence; for therewith a measure is given for the inexhaustible stratification of our nature; and how many who, for one reason or another, believe they have been torn asunder, might not draw from this example of continuability a peculiar consolation.*

(The thought is thrust upon me, that this consolation, too, has somehow found its way into the achievement of the great Elegies, so that they express themselves more completely than, without endangering and rescue, they would have done.) [15]

In 1917 he had written that *only through one of the greatest and innermost renovations it has ever gone through will the world be able to save and maintain itself;* [16] and, two years later, he declared that the task of the intellectual in the post-war world would be *to prepare in men's hearts the way for those gentle, mysterious, trembling transformations, from which alone the understandings and harmonies of a serener future will proceed.*[17] The *Elegies* and the *Sonnets to Orpheus* were Rilke's contributions to this task, and the story of them, which has here been related in some detail, is a proof that the task is possible. This

14 *Briefe an seinen Verleger,* 472, note.
15 *Briefe aus Muzot,* 347–48.
16 *Briefe aus den Jahren 1914–1921,* 165.
17 *Op. cit.,* 247.

primary intention, it is true, was to save himself rather than to save others: his attitude to the old antithesis of self-love and benevolence, in so far as it concerns the artist, is expressed in some words he jotted down on the writing-pad which contains the draft of the last two *Elegies* to be written, the *Tenth* and the *Fifth*: *Art cannot be helpful through our trying to keep and specially concerning ourselves with the distresses of others, but in so far as we bear our own distresses more passionately, give, now and then, a perhaps clearer meaning to endurance, and develop for ourselves the means of expressing the suffering within us and its conquest more precisely and clearly than is possible to those who have to apply their powers to something else.*

II

A word or two may be said about the 'difficulties' of the *Elegies*. To express the matter in its simplest and most general terms, there are really two main difficulties or problems, one of them Rilke's, one of them our own. Rilke's problem was to find symbolic, or what he called 'external,' equivalents for experiences that were becoming ever more 'inward' and incommunicable, and which, when he tried to communicate them, were continually bringing him up against the limitations of language; our problem is to relate these symbols, these 'external equivalents,' to the experiences they symbolise, or (putting the matter less abstractly) to allow their incantation or suggestion to extend our normal consciousness until it is, for a moment, co-extensive with his.

Many readers will recall the description of a certain poet in the *Note-Books of Malte Laurids Brigge*: *Then you set about that unexampled act of violence, your work, which, more and more impatiently, more and more despairingly, sought among visible things equivalents for the vision within.*[18] In his letters we constantly find Rilke regarding external phenomena in this way, as symbols for inner experiences, or—to express the matter a shade more precisely and profoundly—as externality to be internalised and thereby re-created into something existing both within and without. Nature (including all the visible works of man) thus becomes a kind of externalised and visible consciousness, and conscious-

[18] *Gesammelte Werke*, V, 101.

ness a kind of internalised and invisible nature. In 1907 he told his wife that her letters to him from Egypt were like those travel-letters of their grandparents, which were so long in coming and which, when they came, were full of peculiarity and strangeness—except, he added, that to 'us' (as artists, that is to say) all strangeness is akin, *because we conceive of it and require it as expression for something within*.[19] And in the autumn of 1915, during what was, for him, almost the darkest period of the War, he told a young friend, who had written to him of the consolation and refreshment she found in Nature, that Nature had long ceased to be an element into which he could escape and forget: he had for so long been accustomed to regard all existence as a 'task' that some natural sight or scene, in which another might find innocent pleasure and refreshment, simply made new demands upon him, compelling him to try to reproduce it or re-create it within him, to transform it into a symbol or equivalent for some inner experience. *The Spanish landscape (the last I illimitably experienced), Toledo, pushed this tendency of mine to extremes; because there the external thing itself—tower, mountain, bridge—already possessed the unheard of, unsurpassable intensity of those inner equivalents by means of which it might have been represented. Everywhere appearance and vision came, as it were, together in the object, in every one of them a whole inner world was exhibited, as though an angel, in whom space was included, were blind and looking into himself. This world, regarded no longer from the human point of view, but as it is within the angel, is perhaps my real task, one, at any rate, in which all my previous attempts would converge*.[20] Thus, in reading the *Elegies*, we continually find ourselves in a kind of visionary landscape, where things are both familiar and unfamiliar, and where the distinction between inner and outer seems to have been abolished, or transcended.

But even so, remote and unfamiliar as the experience may be, it can only be conveyed by means of words, which, that they may achieve the necessary incantation, must be given, by means of rhythm, emphasis, and context, particular shades and depths of meaning. Here Rilke often finds himself confronted with the limitations of language: sometimes

[19] *Briefe aus den Jahren 1906–1907*, 228.
[20] *Briefe aus den Jahren 1914–1921*, 80.

the particular shade of meaning, the particular tone of feeling he wants a word to bear is not naturally and immediately determined by its particular position; it will only, as Hopkins would say, 'explode' when the reader comes to it with recollections of it in other contexts, even, perhaps, in other works. Sometimes a word or phrase which at first seems puzzling or odd is found to be charged with concentrated or subtle observation of some quite ordinary phenomenon, looked at from Rilke's peculiar angle of vision: we are like amateurs gazing at something through a microscope; at first everything is blurred, but we keep on focussing and adjusting, and then, suddenly, everything is clear. Sometimes a rather special knowledge of portions of the human heritage which had come to possess a symbolic value—the life and poems of Gaspara Stampa and the histories of other 'great lovers,' the legend of Linos, Etruscan tombs, Picasso's *Les Saltimbanques,* Kassner's doctrine of *Umkehr*—is presupposed. Sometimes a knowledge of the author's personal life, in particular of the perpetual conflict he waged between the claims of 'life' and the claims of art, is almost indispensable; for the frequently occurring 'you' (*du*) often means that he is talking to himself, and that what he is saying, although it may possess a general validity, has a particular application. It may thus be objected that there is a certain amount of private language and symbolism in Rilke's later works, and that they lack the universality and immediate recognisability of the greatest poetry, where, although there may be many layers of meaning, what may be called the primary meaning is always immediately apparent. In his defence it may perhaps be pleaded that communication between a modern poet and his audience is much more difficult to establish than it was in simpler and more homogeneous times, especially when the poet is also a prophet, and a prophet, not of any widely accepted system or creed or ideal, but of an intensely personal vision of reality. Indeed, if the reader is prepared to take a little trouble, one may venture to assert that he will soon find the clarity of Rilke's later works far more astonishing than their obscurity, and that he will be perpetually amazed to find a kind of universal validity given to experiences so intensely personal, to conceptions so unfamiliar, to perceptions so subtle, and to intimations so elusive.

Rilke himself, who did so much to extend them, was continually

aware of these limitations of language, and often spoke of them in
letters and conversations. '*Offrande*' *and* '*verger*' *and the word* '*absence*,'
in the great, POSITIVE *sense in which Valéry has used it*, he told a friend,
just after the completion of the *Elegies* and *Sonnets*,—THESE *were, so to
speak, the most painful spots, which sometimes, in the course of the
work, could have made me long for the possibility of comprising all
the advantages of particular languages in one and writing* THEN: *writing*
THEN! [21] *Jacobsen once wrote,* he confided to Frau Wunderly-Volkart,
in 1920, *that he had not liked calling that remarkable story of his that
takes place by the Salzach* '*Two Worlds*'—*again and again he had felt
impelled to say* '*Two World*': *thus one often finds oneself at variance
with the external behaviour of a language and intent on its innermost
life, or on an innermost language, without terminations, if possible,—
a language of word-kernels, a language that's not gathered, up above,
on stalks, but grasped in the speech-seed. Would it not be in this lan-
guage that the perfect Hymn to the Sun would have to be composed,
and isn't the pure silence of love like heart-soil around such speech-seeds?
Oh, how often one longs to speak a few degrees more deeply! My prose
in the* '*Suggested Experiment*' [22] *lies deeper, a shade further in the
ground, than that of Malte, but one gets only a minimal layer further
down; one's left with a mere intimation of the kind of speech that may
be possible* THERE, *where silence reigns.*[23]

[21] Quoted by J. R. von Salis, *Rainer Maria Rilkes Schweizer Jahre*, 99.
[22] The essay *Ur-Geräusch*, referred to in the Commentary on the *Tenth Elegy*, p. 115.
[23] J. R. von Salis, *op. cit.*, 139.

Duino Elegies

AUS DEM BESITZ

DER FÜRSTIN

MARIE VON THURN UND TAXIS-HOHENLOHE

THE PROPERTY OF

PRINCESS

MARIE VON THURN UND TAXIS-HOHENLOHE

Die Erste Elegie

W ER, wenn ich schriee, hörte mich denn aus der Engel
Ordnungen? und gesetzt selbst, es nähme
einer mich plötzlich ans Herz: ich verginge von seinem
stärkeren Dasein. Denn das Schöne ist nichts
als des Schrecklichen Anfang, den wir noch grade ertragen,
und wir bewundern es so, weil es gelassen verschmäht,
uns zu zerstören. Ein jeder Engel ist schrecklich.
Und so verhalt ich mich denn und verschlucke den Lockruf
dunkelen Schluchzens. Ach, wen vermögen
wir denn zu brauchen? Engel nicht, Menschen nicht,   10
und die findigen Tiere merken es schon,
daß wir nicht sehr verläßlich zu Haus sind
in der gedeuteten Welt. Es bleibt uns vielleicht
irgend ein Baum an dem Abhang, daß wir ihn täglich
wiedersähen; es bleibt uns die Straße von gestern
und das verzogene Treusein einer Gewohnheit,
der es bei uns gefiel, und so blieb sie und ging nicht.
O und die Nacht, die Nacht, wenn der Wind voller Weltraum
uns am Angesicht zehrt—, wem bliebe sie nicht, die ersehnte,
sanft enttäuschende, welche dem einzelnen Herzen   20
mühsam bevorsteht. Ist sie den Liebenden leichter?
Ach, sie verdecken sich nur mit einander ihr Los.
Weißt du's n o c h nicht? Wirf aus den Armen die Leere

The First Elegy

Wнo, if I cried, would hear me among the angelic
orders? And even if one of them suddenly
pressed me against his heart, I should fade in the strength of his
stronger existence. For Beauty's nothing
but beginning of Terror we're still just able to bear,
and why we adore it so is because it serenely
disdains to destroy us. Each single angel is terrible.
And so I keep down my heart, and swallow the call-note
of depth-dark sobbing. Alas, who is there
we can make use of? Not angels, not men;   10
and already the knowing brutes are aware
that we don't feel very securely at home
within our interpreted world. There remains, perhaps,
some tree on a slope, to be looked at day after day,
there remains for us yesterday's walk and the cupboard-love loyalty
of a habit that liked us and stayed and never gave notice.
Oh, and there's Night, there's Night, when wind full of cosmic space
feeds on our faces: for whom would she not remain,
longed for, mild disenchantress, painfully there
for the lonely heart to achieve? Is she lighter for lovers?   20
Alas, with each other they only conceal their lot!
Don't you know *yet*?—Fling the emptiness out of your arms

zu den Räumen hinzu, die wir atmen; vielleicht daß die Vögel
die erweiterte Luft fühlen mit innigerm Flug.

Ja, die Frühlinge brauchten dich wohl. Es muteten manche
Sterne dir zu, daß du sie spürtest. Es hob
sich eine Woge heran im Vergangenen, oder
da du vorüberkamst am geöffneten Fenster,
gab eine Geige sich hin. Das alles war Auftrag.   30
Aber bewältigtest du's? Warst du nicht immer
noch von Erwartung zerstreut, als kündigte alles
eine Geliebte dir an? (Wo willst du sie bergen,
da doch die großen fremden Gedanken bei dir
aus und ein gehn und öfters bleiben bei Nacht.)
Sehnt es dich aber, so singe die Liebenden; lange
noch nicht unsterblich genug ist ihr berühmtes Gefühl.
Jene, du neidest sie fast, Verlassenen, die du
so viel liebender fandst als die Gestillten. Beginn
immer von neuem die nie zu erreichende Preisung;   40
denk: es erhält sich der Held, selbst der Untergang war ihm
nur ein Vorwand, zu sein: seine letzte Geburt.
Aber die Liebenden nimmt die erschöpfte Natur
in sich zurück, als wären nicht zweimal die Kräfte,
dieses zu leisten. Hast du der Gaspara Stampa
denn genügend gedacht, daß irgend ein Mädchen,
dem der Geliebte entging, am gesteigerten Beispiel
dieser Liebenden fühlt: daß ich würde wie sie?
Sollen nicht endlich uns diese ältesten Schmerzen
fruchtbarer werden? Ist es nicht Zeit, daß wir liebend   50
uns vom Geliebten befrein und es bebend bestehn:
wie der Pfeil die Sehne besteht, um gesammelt im Absprung
m e h r zu sein als er selbst. Denn Bleiben ist nirgends.

Stimmen, Stimmen. Höre, mein Herz, wie sonst nur
Heilige hörten: daß sie der riesige Ruf

into the spaces we breathe—maybe that the birds
will feel the extended air in more intimate flight.

Yes, the Springs had need of you. Many a star
was waiting for you to espy it. Many a wave
would rise on the past towards you; or, else, perhaps,
as you went by an open window, a violin
would be giving itself to someone. All this was a trust.
But were you equal to it? Were you not always   30
distracted by expectation, as though all this
were announcing someone to love? (As if you could hope
to conceal her, with all those great strange thoughts
going in and out and often staying overnight!)
No, when longing comes over you, sing the great lovers: the fame
of all they can feel is far from immortal enough.
Those whom you almost envied, those forsaken, you found
so far beyond the requited in loving. Begin
ever anew their never attainable praise.
Consider: the Hero continues, even his fall   40
was a pretext for further existence, an ultimate birth.
But lovers are taken back by exhausted Nature
into herself, as though such creative force
could never be re-exerted. Have you so fully remembranced
Gaspara Stampa, that any girl, whose beloved's
eluded her, may feel, from that far intenser
example of loving: "if I could become like her!"?
Ought not these oldest sufferings of ours to be yielding
more fruit by now? Is it not time that, in loving,
we freed ourselves from the loved one, and, quivering, endured: 50
as the arrow endures the string, to become, in the gathering out-leap,
something more than itself? For staying is nowhere.

Voices, voices. Hear, O my heart, as only
saints have heard: heard till the giant-call

aufhob vom Boden; sie aber knieten,
Unmögliche, weiter und achtetens nicht:
S o waren sie hörend. Nicht daß du Gottes ertrügest
die Stimme, bei weitem. Aber das Wehende höre,
die ununterbrochene Nachricht, die aus Stille sich bildet.   60
Es rauscht jetzt von jenen jungen Toten zu dir.
Wo immer du eintratst, redete nicht in Kirchen
zu Rom und Neapel ruhig ihr Schicksal dich an?
Oder es trug eine Inschrift sich erhaben dir auf,
wie neulich die Tafel in Santa Maria Formosa.
Was sie mir wollen? leise soll ich des Unrechts
Anschein abtun, der ihrer Geister
reine Bewegung manchmal ein wenig behindert.

Freilich ist es seltsam, die Erde nicht mehr zu bewohnen,
kaum erlernte Gebräuche nicht mehr zu üben,   70
Rosen, und andern eigens versprechenden Dingen
nicht die Bedeutung menschlicher Zukunft zu geben;
das, was man war in unendlich ängstlichen Händen,
nicht mehr zu sein, und selbst den eigenen Namen
wegzulassen wie ein zerbrochenes Spielzeug.
Seltsam, die Wünsche nicht weiterzuwünschen. Seltsam,
alles, was sich bezog, so lose im Raume
flattern zu sehen. Und das Totsein ist mühsam
und voller Nachholn, daß man allmählich ein wenig
Ewigkeit spürt.—Aber Lebendige machen   80
alle den Fehler, daß sie zu stark unterscheiden.
Engel (sagt man) wüßten oft nicht, ob sie unter
Lebenden gehn oder Toten. Die ewige Strömung
reißt durch beide Bereiche alle Alter
immer mit sich und übertönt sie in beiden.

Schließlich brauchen sie uns nicht mehr, die Früheentrückten,
man entwöhnt sich des Irdischen sanft, wie man den Brüsten

lifted them off the ground; yet they went impossibly
on with their kneeling, in undistracted attention:
so inherently hearers. Not that you could endure
the voice of God—far from it. But hark to the suspiration,
the uninterrupted news that grows out of silence.
Rustling towards you now from those youthfully-dead.
Whenever you entered a church in Rome or in Naples
were you not always being quietly addressed by their fate?
Or else an inscription sublimely imposed itself on you,
as, lately, the tablet in Santa Maria Formosa.
What they require of me? I must gently remove the appearance
of suffered injustice, that hinders
a little, at times, their purely-proceeding spirits.

True, it is strange to inhabit the earth no longer,
to use no longer customs scarcely acquired,
not to interpret roses, and other things
that promise so much, in terms of a human future;
to be no longer all that one used to be
in endlessly anxious hands, and to lay aside
even one's proper name like a broken toy.
Strange, not to go on wishing one's wishes. Strange,
to see all that was once relation so loosely fluttering
hither and thither in space. And it's hard, being dead,
and full of retrieving before one begins to espy
a trace of eternity.—Yes, but all of the living
make the mistake of drawing too sharp distinctions.
Angels, (they say) are often unable to tell
whether they move among living or dead. The eternal
torrent whirls all the ages through either realm
for ever, and sounds above their voices in both.

They've finally no more need of us, the early-departed,
one's gently weaned from terrestrial things as one mildly

milde der Mutter entwächst. Aber wir, die so große
Geheimnisse brauchen, denen aus Trauer so oft
seliger Fortschritt entspringt—: k ö n n t e n wir sein ohne sie?   90
Ist die Sage umsonst, daß einst in der Klage um Linos
wagende erste Musik dürre Erstarrung durchdrang,
daß erst im erschrockenen Raum, dem ein beinah göttlicher Jüngling
plötzlich für immer enttrat, das Leere in jene
Schwingung geriet, die uns jetzt hinreißt und tröstet und hilft.

outgrows the breasts of a mother. But we, that have need of
such mighty secrets, we, for whom sorrow's so often
source of blessedest progress, could we exist without them?
Is the story in vain, how once, in the mourning for Linos,
venturing earliest music pierced barren numbness, and how,
in the horrified space an almost deified youth
suddenly quitted for ever, emptiness first
felt the vibration that now charms us and comforts and helps?

Die Zweite Elegie

JEDER Engel ist schrecklich. Und dennoch, weh mir,
ansing ich euch, fast tödliche Vögel der Seele,
wissend um euch. Wohin sind die Tage Tobiae,
da der Strahlendsten einer stand an der einfachen Haustür,
zur Reise ein wenig verkleidet und schon nicht mehr furchtbar;
(Jüngling dem Jüngling, wie er neugierig hinaussah).
Träte der Erzengel jetzt, der gefährliche, hinter den Sternen
eines Schrittes nur nieder und herwärts: hochauf-
schlagend erschlüg uns das eigene Herz. Wer seid ihr?

Frühe Geglückte, ihr Verwöhnten der Schöpfung,   10
Höhenzüge, morgenrötliche Grate
aller Erschaffung,—Pollen der blühenden Gottheit,
Gelenke des Lichtes, Gänge, Treppen, Throne,
Räume aus Wesen, Schilde aus Wonne, Tumulte
stürmisch entzückten Gefühls und plötzlich, einzeln,
Spiegel: die die entströmte eigene Schönheit
wiederschöpfen zurück in das eigene Antlitz.

Denn wir, wo wir fühlen, verflüchtigen; ach wir
atmen uns aus und dahin; von Holzglut zu Holzglut
geben wir schwächern Geruch. Da sagt uns wohl einer: 20
ja, du gehst mir ins Blut, dieses Zimmer, der Frühling

The Second Elegy

Every Angel is terrible. Still, though, alas!
  I invoke you, almost deadly birds of the soul,
  knowing what you are. Oh, where are the days of Tobias,
when one of the shining-most stood on the simple threshold,
a little disguised for the journey, no longer appalling,
(a youth to the youth as he curiously peered outside).
Let the archangel perilous now, from behind the stars,
step but a step down hitherwards: high up-beating,
our heart would out-beat us. Who are you?

Early successes, Creation's pampered darlings,   10
ranges, summits, dawn-red ridges
of all beginning,—pollen of blossoming godhead,
hinges of light, corridors, stairways, thrones,
spaces of being, shields of felicity, tumults
of stormily-rapturous feeling, and suddenly, separate,
mirrors, drawing up their own
outstreamed beauty into their faces again.

For we, when we feel, evaporate; oh, we
breathe ourselves out and away; from ember to ember
yielding a fainter scent. True, someone may tell us: 20
'You've got in my blood, the room, the Spring's

füllt sich mit dir . . . Was hilfts, er kann uns nicht halten,
wir schwinden in ihm und um ihn. Und jene, die schön sind,
o wer hält sie zurück? Unaufhörlich steht Anschein
auf in ihrem Gesicht und geht fort. Wie Tau von dem Frühgras
hebt sich das Unsre von uns, wie die Hitze von einem
heißen Gericht. O Lächeln, wohin? O Aufschaun:
neue, warme, entgehende Welle des Herzens—;
weh mir: wir s i n d s doch. Schmeckt denn der Weltraum,
in den wir uns lösen, nach uns? Fangen die Engel   30
wirklich nur Ihriges auf, ihnen Entströmtes,
oder ist manchmal, wie aus Versehen, ein wenig
unseres Wesens dabei? Sind wir in ihre
Züge soviel nur gemischt wie das Vage in die Gesichter
schwangerer Frauen? Sie merken es nicht in dem Wirbel
ihrer Rückkehr zu sich. (Wie sollten sie's merken.)

Liebende könnten, verstünden sie's, in der Nachtluft
wunderlich reden. Denn es scheint, daß uns alles
verheimlicht. Siehe, die Bäume s i n d; die Häuser,
die wir bewohnen, bestehn noch. Wir nur   40
ziehen allem vorbei wie ein luftiger Austausch.
Und alles ist einig, uns zu verschweigen, halb als
Schande vielleicht und halb als unsägliche Hoffnung.

Liebende, euch, ihr in einander Genügten,
frag ich nach uns. Ihr greift euch. Habt ihr Beweise?
Seht, mir geschiehts, daß meine Hände einander
inne werden oder daß mein gebrauchtes
Gesicht in ihnen sich schont. Das gibt mir ein wenig
Empfindung. Doch wer wagte darum schon zu s e i n?
Ihr aber, die ihr im Entzücken des anderen   50
zunehmt, bis er euch überwältigt
anfleht: nicht m e h r—; die ihr unter den Händen
euch reichlicher werdet wie Traubenjahre;

growing full of you' . . . What's the use? He cannot retain us.
We vanish within and around him. And those that have beauty,
oh, who shall hold them back? Incessant appearance
comes and goes in their faces. Like dew from the morning grass
exhales from us that which is ours, like heat
from a smoking dish. O smile, whither? O upturned glance:
new, warm, vanishing wave of the heart—alas,
but we *are* all that. Does the cosmic space
we dissolve into taste of us, then? Do the angels really   30
only catch up what is theirs, what has streamed from them, or at times,
as though through an oversight, is a little of our
existence in it as well? Is there just so much of us
mixed with their features as that vague look in the faces
of pregnant women? Unmarked by them in their whirling
return to themselves. (How should they remark it?)

Lovers, if Angels could understand them, might utter
strange things in the midnight air. For it seems that everything's
trying to hide us. Look, the trees exist; the houses
we live in still stand where they were. We only   40
pass everything by like a transposition of air.
And all combines to suppress us, partly as shame,
perhaps, and partly as inexpressible hope.

Lovers, to you, each satisfied in the other,
I turn with my question about us. You grasp yourselves. Have you proofs?
Look, with me it may happen at times that my hands
grow aware of each other, or else that my hard-worn face
seeks refuge within them. That gives me a little
sensation. But who, just for that, could presume to exist?
You, though, that go on growing   50
in the other's rapture till, overwhelmed, he implores
'No more'; you that under each other's hands
grow more abundant like vintage grapes;

die ihr manchmal vergeht, nur weil der andre
ganz überhand nimmt: euch frag ich nach uns. Ich weiß,
ihr berührt euch so selig, weil die Liebkosung verhält,
weil die Stelle nicht schwindet, die ihr, Zärtliche,
zudeckt; weil ihr darunter das reine
Dauern verspürt. So versprecht ihr euch Ewigkeit fast
von der Umarmung. Und doch, wenn ihr der ersten   60
Blicke Schrecken besteht und die Sehnsucht am Fenster
und den ersten gemeinsamen Gang, e i n Mal durch den Garten:
Liebende, s e i d ihrs dann noch? Wenn ihr einer dem andern
euch an den Mund hebt und ansetzt—: Getränk an Getränk:
o wie entgeht dann der Trinkende seltsam der Handlung.

Erstaunte euch nicht auf attischen Stelen die Vorsicht
menschlicher Geste? war nicht Liebe und Abschied
so leicht auf die Schultern gelegt, als wär es aus anderm
Stoffe gemacht als bei uns? Gedenkt euch der Hände,
wie sie drucklos beruhen, obwohl in den Torsen die Kraft steht.   70
Diese Beherrschten wußten damit: so weit sind wirs,
dieses ist unser, uns s o zu berühren; stärker
stemmen die Götter uns an. Doch dies ist Sache der Götter.
Fänden auch wir ein reines, verhaltenes, schmales
Menschliches, einen unseren Streifen Fruchtlands
zwischen Strom und Gestein. Denn das eigene Herz übersteigt **uns**
noch immer wie jene. Und wir können ihm nicht mehr
nachschaun in Bilder, die es besänftigen, noch in
göttliche Körper, in denen es größer sich mäßigt.

sinking at times, but only because the other
has so completely emerged; I ask you about us. I know
why you so blissfully touch: because the caress persists,
because it does not vanish, the place that you
so tenderly cover; because you perceive thereunder
pure duration. Until your embraces almost
promise eternity. Yet, when you've once withstood
the startled first encounter, the window-longing,
and that first walk, just once, through the garden together:
Lovers, are you the same? When you lift yourselves
up to each other's lips—drink unto drink:
oh, how strangely the drinker eludes his part!

On Attic stelês, did not the circumspection
of human gesture amaze you? Were not love and farewell
so lightly laid upon shoulders, they seemed to be made
of other stuff than with us? Remember the hands,
how they rest without pressure, though power is there in the torsos.
The wisdom of those self-masters was this: we have got so far;
ours is to touch one another like this; the gods
may press more strongly upon us. But that is the gods' affair.
If only we could discover some pure, contained,
narrow, human, own little strip of orchard
in between river and rock! For our heart transcends us
just as it did those others. And we can no longer
gaze after it into figures that soothe it, or godlike
bodies, wherein it achieves a grander restraint.

Die Dritte Elegie

Eines ist, die Geliebte zu singen. Ein anderes, wehe,
jenen verborgenen schuldigen Fluß-Gott des Bluts.
Den sie von weitem erkennt, ihren Jüngling, was weiß er
selbst von dem Herren der Lust, der aus dem Einsamen oft,
ehe das Mädchen noch linderte, oft auch als wäre sie nicht,
ach, von welchem Unkenntlichen triefend, das Gotthaupt
aufhob, aufrufend die Nacht zu unendlichem Aufruhr.
O des Blutes Neptun, o sein furchtbarer Dreizack.
O der dunkele Wind seiner Brust aus gewundener Muschel.
Horch, wie die Nacht sich muldet und höhlt. Ihr Sterne,
stammt nicht von euch des Liebenden Lust zu dem Antlitz
seiner Geliebten? Hat er die innige Einsicht
in ihr reines Gesicht nicht aus dem reinen Gestirn?

Du nicht hast ihm, wehe, nicht seine Mutter
hat ihm die Bogen der Braun so zur Erwartung gespannt.
Nicht an dir, ihn fühlendes Mädchen, an dir nicht
bog seine Lippe sich zum fruchtbarern Ausdruck.
Meinst du wirklich, ihn hätte dein leichter Auftritt
also erschüttert, du, die wandelt wie Frühwind?
Zwar du erschrakst ihm das Herz; doch ältere Schrecken
stürzten in ihn bei dem berührenden Anstoß.
Ruf ihn . . . du rufst ihn nicht ganz aus dunkelem Umgang.

The Third Elegy

ONE thing to sing the beloved, another, alas!
that hidden guilty river-god of the blood.
He whom she knows from afar, her lover, what does he know
of that Lord of Pleasure, who often, out of his lonely heart,
before she had soothed him, often as though she did not exist,
streaming from, oh, what unknowable depths, would uplift
his god-head, uprousing the night to infinite uproar?
Oh, the Neptune within our blood, oh, his terrible trident!
Oh, the gloomy blast of his breast from the twisted shell!
Hark, how the night grows fluted and hollowed. You stars,   10
is it not from you that the lover's delight in the loved one's
face arises? Does not his intimate insight
into her purest face come from the purest star?

It was not you, alas! It was not his mother
that bent his brows into such an expectant arch.
Not to meet yours, girl feeling him, not to meet yours
did his lips begin to assume that more fruitful curve.
Do you really suppose your gentle approach could have so
convulsed him, you, that wander like morning-breezes?
You terrified his heart, indeed; but more ancient terrors   20
rushed into him in that instant of shattering contact.
Call him . . . you can't quite call him away from those sombre companions.

Freilich, er w i l l, er entspringt; erleichtert gewöhnt er
sich in dein heimliches Herz und nimmt und beginnt sich.
Aber begann er sich je?
Mutter, d u machtest ihn klein, du warsts, die ihn anfing;
dir war er neu, du beugtest über die neuen
Augen die freundliche Welt und wehrtest der fremden.
Wo, ach, hin sind die Jahre, da du ihm einfach
mit der schlanken Gestalt wallendes Chaos vertratst?   30
Vieles verbargst du ihm so; das nächtlich verdächtige Zimmer
machtest du harmlos, aus deinem Herzen voll Zuflucht
mischtest du menschlichern Raum seinem Nacht-Raum hinzu.
Nicht in die Finsternis, nein, in dein näheres Dasein
hast du das Nachtlicht gestellt, und es schien wie aus Freundschaft.
Nirgends ein Knistern, das du nicht lächelnd erklärtest,
so als wüßtest du längst, w a n n sich die Diele benimmt . . .
Und er horchte und linderte sich. So vieles vermochte
zärtlich dein Aufstehn; hinter den Schrank trat
hoch im Mantel sein Schicksal, und in die Falten des Vorhangs   40
paßte, die leicht sich verschob, seine unruhige Zukunft.

Und er selbst, wie er lag, der Erleichterte, unter
schläfernden Lidern deiner leichten Gestaltung
Süße lösend in den gekosteten Vorschlaf—:
s c h i e n ein Gehüteter . . . Aber i n n e n: wer wehrte,
hinderte innen in ihm die Fluten der Herkunft?
Ach, da w a r keine Vorsicht im Schlafenden; schlafend,
aber träumend, aber in Fiebern: wie er sich einließ.
Er, der Neue, Scheuende, wie er verstrickt war,
mit des innern Geschehns weiterschlagenden Ranken   50
schon zu Mustern verschlungen, zu würgendem Wachstum, zu tierhaft
jagenden Formen. Wie er sich hingab—. Liebte.
Liebte sein Inneres, seines Inneren Wildnis,
diesen Urwald in ihm, auf dessen stummem Gestürztsein
lichtgrün sein Herz stand. Liebte. Verließ es, ging die

Truly, he tries to, he does escape them; disburdenedly settles
into your intimate heart, receives and begins himself there.
Did he ever begin himself, though?
Mother, you made him small, it was you that began him;
he was new to you, you arched over those new eyes
the friendly world, averting the one that was strange.
Where, oh where, are the years when you simply displaced
for him, with your slender figure, the surging abyss?   30
You hid so much from him then; made the nightly-suspected room
harmless, and out of your heart full of refuge
mingled more human space with that of his nights.
Not in the darkness, no, but within your far nearer presence
you placed the light, and it shone as though out of friendship.
Nowhere a creak you could not explain with a smile,
as though you had long known *when* the floor would behave itself thus . . .
And he listened to you and was soothed. So much it availed,
gently, your coming; his tall cloaked destiny stepped
behind the chest of drawers, and his restless future,   40
that easily got out of place, conformed to the folds of the curtain.

And he himself as he lay there in such relief,
mingling, under his drowsy eyelids, the sweetness
of your light shaping with foretaste of coming sleep,
seemed to be under protection . . . Within, though: who could avert,
divert, the floods of origin flowing within him?
Alas! there *was* no caution within that sleeper; sleeping,
yes, but dreaming, yes, but feverish: what he embarked on!
He, so new, so timorous, how he got tangled
in ever-encroaching roots of inner event,   50
twisted to primitive patterns, to throttling growths, to bestial
preying forms! How he gave himself up to it! Loved.
Loved his interior world, his interior jungle,
that primal forest within, on whose mute overthrownness,
green-lit, his heart stood. Loved. Left it, continued

eigenen Wurzeln hinaus in gewaltigen Ursprung,
wo seine kleine Geburt schon überlebt war. Liebend
stieg er hinab in das ältere Blut, in die Schluchten,
wo das Furchtbare lag, noch satt von den Vätern. Und jedes
Schreckliche kannte ihn, blinzelte, war wie verständigt.   60
Ja, das Entsetzliche lächelte . . . Selten
hast du so zärtlich gelächelt, Mutter. Wie sollte
er es nicht lieben, da es ihm lächelte. V o r dir
hat ers geliebt, denn, da du ihn trugst schon,
war es im Wasser gelöst, das den Keimenden leicht macht.

Siehe, wir lieben nicht, wie die Blumen, aus einem
einzigen Jahr; uns steigt, wo wir lieben,
unvordenklicher Saft in die Arme. O Mädchen,
dies: daß wir liebten i n uns, nicht Eines, ein Künftiges, sondern
das zahllos Brauende; nicht ein einzelnes Kind,   70
sondern die Väter, die wie Trümmer Gebirgs
uns im Grunde beruhn; sondern das trockene Flußbett
einstiger Mütter—; sondern die ganze
lautlose Landschaft unter dem wolkigen oder
reinen Verhängnis—: d i e s kam dir, Mädchen, zuvor.

Und du selber, was weißt du—, du locktest
Vorzeit empor in dem Liebenden. Welche Gefühle
wühlten herauf aus entwandelten Wesen. Welche
Frauen haßten dich da. Wasfür finstere Männer
regtest du auf im Geäder des Jünglings? Tote   80
Kinder wollten zu dir . . . O leise, leise,
tu ein liebes vor ihm, ein verläßliches Tagwerk,—führ ihn
nah an den Garten heran, gib ihm der Nächte
Übergewicht . . . . . .
                        Verhalt ihn . . . . . .

into his own roots and out into violent beginning
where his tiny birth was already outlived. Descended,
lovingly, into the older blood, the ravines
where Frightfulness lurked, still gorged with his fathers. And every
terror knew him, and winked, and quite understood.   60
Yes, Horror smiled at him . . . Seldom
did you, Mother, smile so tenderly. How could he help
loving what smiled at him? Long before you
he loved it, for, even while you bore him,
it was there, dissolved in the water that lightens the seed.

Look, we don't love like flowers, with only a single
season behind us; immemorial sap
mounts in our arms when we love. Oh, maid,
this: that we've loved, *within* us, not one, still to come, but all
the innumerable fermentation; not just a single child,   70
but the fathers, resting like mountain-ruins
within our depths;—but the dry river-bed
of former mothers;—yes, and the whole of that
soundless landscape under its cloudy or
cloudless destiny:—*this* got the start of you, maid.

And you yourself, how can you tell,—you have conjured up
prehistoric time in your lover. What feelings
whelmed up from beings gone by! What women
hated you in him! What sinister men
you roused in his youthful veins! Dead children   80
were trying to reach you . . . Oh gently, gently
show him daily a loving, confident task done,—guide him
close to the garden, give him those counter-
balancing nights . . . . . .
          Withhold him . . . . . .

Die Vierte Elegie

O BÄUME Lebens, o wann winterlich?
Wir sind nicht einig. Sind nicht wie die Zug-
vögel verständigt. Überholt und spät,
so drängen wir uns plötzlich Winden auf
und fallen ein auf teilnahmslosen Teich.
Blühn und verdorrn ist uns zugleich bewußt.
Und irgendwo gehn Löwen noch und wissen,
solang sie herrlich sind, von keiner Ohnmacht.

Uns aber, wo wir Eines meinen, ganz,
ist schon des andern Aufwand fühlbar. Feindschaft   10
ist uns das Nächste. Treten Liebende
nicht immerfort an Ränder, eins im andern,
die sich versprachen Weite, Jagd und Heimat.
Da wird für eines Augenblickes Zeichnung
ein Grund von Gegenteil bereitet, mühsam,
daß wir sie sähen; denn man ist sehr deutlich
mit uns. Wir kennen den Kontur
des Fühlens nicht, nur was ihn formt von außen.
Wer saß nicht bang vor seines Herzens Vorhang?
Der schlug sich auf: die Szenerie war Abschied.   20
Leicht zu verstehen. Der bekannte Garten,
und schwankte leise: dann erst kam der Tänzer.

The Fourth Elegy

O TREES of life, when will your winter come?
    We're never single-minded, unperplexed,
    like migratory birds. Outstript and late,
we suddenly thrust into the wind, and fall
into unfeeling ponds. We comprehend
flowering and fading simultaneously.
And somewhere lions still roam, all unaware,
in being magnificent, of any weakness.

We, though, while we're intent upon one thing,
can feel the cost and conquest of another.   10
Hostility's our first response. Aren't lovers
for ever reaching verges in each other,—
lovers, that looked for spaces, hunting, home?
Then, for the sudden sketchwork of a moment,
a ground of contrast's painfully prepared,
to make us see it. For they're very clear
with us, we that don't know our feeling's shape,
but only that which forms it from outside.
Who's not sat tense before his own heart's curtain?
Up it would go: the scenery was parting.   20
Easy to understand. The well-known garden,
swaying a little. Then appeared the dancer

Nicht d e r. Genug. Und wenn er auch so leicht tut,
er ist verkleidet und er wird ein Bürger
und geht durch seine Küche in die Wohnung.
Ich will nicht diese halbgefüllten Masken,
lieber die Puppe. Die ist voll. Ich will
den Balg aushalten und den Draht und ihr
Gesicht aus Aussehn. Hier. Ich bin davor.
Wenn auch die Lampen ausgehn, wenn mir auch   30
gesagt wird: Nichts mehr—, wenn auch von der Bühne
das Leere herkommt mit dem grauen Luftzug,
wenn auch von meinen stillen Vorfahrn keiner
mehr mit mir dasitzt, keine Frau, sogar
der Knabe nicht mehr mit dem braunen Schielaug:
Ich bleibe dennoch. Es gibt immer Zuschaun.

Hab ich nicht recht? Du, der um mich so bitter
das Leben schmeckte, meines kostend, Vater,
den ersten trüben Aufguß meines Müssens,
da ich heranwuchs, immer wieder kostend   40
und, mit dem Nachgeschmack so fremder Zukunft
beschäftigt, prüftest mein beschlagnes Aufschaun,—
der du, mein Vater, seit du tot bist, oft
in meiner Hoffnung innen in mir Angst hast,
und Gleichmut, wie ihn Tote haben, Reiche
von Gleichmut, aufgibst für mein bißchen Schicksal,
hab ich nicht recht? Und ihr, hab ich nicht recht,
die ihr mich liebtet für den kleinen Anfang
Liebe zu euch, von dem ich immer abkam,
weil mir der Raum in eurem Angesicht,   50
da ich ihn liebte, überging in Weltraum,
in dem ihr nicht mehr wart . . . Wenn mir zumut ist,
zu warten vor der Puppenbühne, nein,
so völlig hinzuschaun, daß, um mein Schauen
am Ende aufzuwiegen, dort als Spieler

Not *the* Enough! However light he foots it,
he's just disguised, and turns into a bourgeois,
and passes through the kitchen to his dwelling.
I will not have those half-filled masks! No, no,
rather the doll. That's full. I'll force myself
to bear the husk, the wire, and even the face
that's all outside. Here! I'm already waiting.
Even if the lights go out, even if I'm told   30
'There's nothing more,'—even if greyish draughts
of emptiness come drifting from the stage,—
even if of all my silent forebears none
sits by me any longer, not a woman,
not even the boy with the brown squinting eyes:
I'll still remain. For one can always watch.

Am I not right? You, to whom life would taste
so bitter, Father, when you tasted mine,
that turbid first infusion of my Must,
you kept on tasting as I kept on growing,   40
and, fascinated by the after-taste
of such queer future, tried my clouded gaze,—
you, who so often since you died, my Father,
have been afraid within my inmost hope,
surrendering realms of that serenity
the dead are lords of for my bit of fate,—
am I not right? And you, am I not right,—
you that would love me for that small beginning
of love for you I always turned away from,
because the space within your faces changed,   50
even while I loved it, into cosmic space
where you no longer were . . . , when I feel like it,
to wait before the puppet stage,—no, rather
gaze so intensely on it that at last,
to upweigh my gaze, an angel has to come

ein Engel hinmuß, der die Bälge hochreißt.
Engel und Puppe: dann ist endlich Schauspiel.
Dann kommt zusammen, was wir immerfort
entzwein, indem wir da sind. Dann entsteht
aus unsern Jahreszeiten erst der Umkreis   60
des ganzen Wandelns. Über uns hinüber
spielt dann der Engel. Sieh, die Sterbenden,
sollten sie nicht vermuten, wie voll Vorwand
das alles ist, was wir hier leisten. Alles
ist nicht es selbst. O Stunden in der Kindheit,
da hinter den Figuren mehr als nur
Vergangnes war und vor uns nicht die Zukunft.
Wir wuchsen freilich und wir drängten manchmal,
bald groß zu werden, denen halb zulieb,
die andres nicht mehr hatten, als das Großsein.   70
Und waren doch in unserem Alleingehn
mit Dauerndem vergnügt und standen da
im Zwischenraume zwischen Welt und Spielzeug,
an einer Stelle, die seit Anbeginn
gegründet war für einen reinen Vorgang.

Wer zeigt ein Kind, so wie es steht? Wer stellt
es ins Gestirn und gibt das Maß des Abstands
ihm in die Hand? Wer macht den Kindertod
aus grauem Brot, das hart wird,—oder läßt
ihn drin im runden Mund so wie den Gröps   80
von einem schönen Apfel? . . . . Mörder sind
leicht einzusehen. Aber dies: den Tod,
den ganzen Tod, noch v o r dem Leben so
sanft zu enthalten und nicht bös zu sein,
ist unbeschreiblich.

and play a part there, snatching up the husks?
Angel and doll! Then there's at last a play.
Then there unites what we continually
part by our being there. Then at last
can spring from our own turning years the cycle   60
of the whole going-on. Over and above us
there's then the angel playing. Look, the dying,—
surely they must suspect how full of pretext
is all that we accomplish here, where nothing
is what it really is. O hours of childhood,
hours when behind the figures there was more
than the mere past, and when what lay before us
was not the future! We were growing, and sometimes
impatient to grow up, half for the sake
of those who'd nothing left but their grown-upness.   70
Yet, when alone, we entertained ourselves
with everlastingness: there we would stand,
within the gap left between world and toy,
upon a spot which, from the first beginning,
had been established for a pure event.

Who'll show a child just as it is? Who'll place it
within its constellation, with the measure
of distance in its hand? Who'll make its death
from grey bread, that grows hard,—or leave it there,
within the round mouth, like the choking core   80
of a sweet apple? . . . . . . Minds of murderers
are easily divined. But this, though: death,
the whole of death,—even before life's begun,
to hold it all so gently, and be good:
this is beyond description!

Die Fünfte Elegie

Frau Hertha Koenig zugeeignet

WER aber s i n d sie, sag mir, die Fahrenden, diese ein wenig
Flüchtigern noch als wir selbst, die dringend von früh an
wringt ein wem—wem zuliebe
niemals zufriedener Wille? Sondern er wringt sie,
biegt sie, schlingt sie und schwingt sie,
wirft sie und fängt sie zurück; wie aus geölter,
glatterer Luft kommen sie nieder
auf dem verzehrten, von ihrem ewigen
Aufsprung dünneren Teppich, diesem verlorenen
Teppich im Weltall.   10
Aufgelegt wie ein Pflaster, als hätte der Vorstadt-
Himmel der Erde dort wehegetan.
                                    Und kaum dort,
aufrecht, da und gezeigt: des Dastehns
großer Anfangsbuchstab . . . , schon auch, die stärksten
Männer, rollt sie wieder, zum Scherz, der immer
kommende Griff, wie August der Starke bei Tisch
einen zinnenen Teller.

Ach und um diese
Mitte, die Rose des Zuschauns: 20

The Fifth Elegy

Dedicated to Frau Hertha von Koenig

B<small>UT</small> tell me, who *are* they, these acrobats, even a little
   more fleeting than we ourselves,—so urgently, ever since childhood,
   wrung by an (oh, for the sake of whom?)
never-contented will? That keeps on wringing them,
bending them, slinging them, swinging them,
throwing them and catching them back; as though from an oily
smoother air, they come down on the threadbare
carpet, thinned by their everlasting
upspringing, this carpet forlornly
lost in the cosmos.   10
Laid on there like a plaster, as though the suburban
sky had injured the earth.
                  And hardly there,
upright, shown there: the great initial
letter of Thereness,—then even the strongest
men are rolled once more, in sport, by the ever-
returning grasp, as once by Augustus the Strong
a tin platter at table.

Alas, and round this
centre the rose of onlooking   20

-< 47 >-

blüht und entblättert. Um diesen
Stampfer, den Stempel, den von dem eignen
blühenden Staub getroffen, zur Scheinfrucht
wieder der Unlust befruchteten, ihrer
niemals bewußten,—glänzend mit dünnster
Oberfläche leicht scheinlächelnden Unlust.

Da, der welke, faltige Stemmer,
der alte, der nur noch trommelt,
eingegangen in seiner gewaltigen Haut, als hätte sie früher
z w e i Männer enthalten, und einer
läge nun schon auf dem Kirchhof, und er überlebte den andern,   30
taub und manchmal ein wenig
wirr, in der verwitweten Haut.

Aber der junge, der Mann, als wär er der Sohn eines Nackens
und einer Nonne: prall und strammig erfüllt
mit Muskeln und Einfalt.

Oh ihr,
die ein Leid, das noch klein war,
einst als Spielzeug bekam, in einer seiner
langen Genesungen   40

Du, der mit dem Aufschlag,
wie nur Früchte ihn kennen, unreif
täglich hundert Mal abfällt vom Baum der gemeinsam
erbauten Bewegung, (der, rascher als Wasser, in wenig
Minuten Lenz, Sommer und Herbst hat)—
abfällt und anprallt ans Grab:
manchmal, in halber Pause, will dir ein liebes
Antlitz entstehn hinüber zu deiner selten
zärtlichen Mutter; doch an deinen Körper verliert sich,
der es flächig verbraucht, das schüchtern   50

blooms and unblossoms. Round this
pestle, this pistil, caught by its own
dust-pollen, and fertilised over again
to a sham-fruit of boredom, their own
never-realised boredom, gleaming with thinnest
lightly sham-smiling surface.

There, the withered wrinkled lifter,
old now and only drumming,
shrivelled up in his mighty skin as though it had once contained
two men, and one were already   30
lying in the churchyard, and he had outlasted the other,
deaf and sometimes a little
strange in his widowed skin.

And the youngster, the man, like the son of a neck
and a nun: so tautly and smartly filled
with muscle and simpleness.

O you,
a pain that was still quite small
received as a plaything once in one of its
long convalescences. . . .   40

You, that fall with the thud
only fruits know, unripe,
daily a hundred times from the tree
of mutually built up motion (the tree that, swifter than water,
has spring and summer and autumn in so many minutes),
fall and rebound on the grave:
sometimes, in half-pauses, a tenderness tries
to steal out over your face to your seldomly
tender mother, but scatters over your body,
whose surface quickly absorbs the timidly rippling,   50

kaum versuchte Gesicht . . . Und wieder
klatscht der Mann in die Hand zu dem Ansprung, und eh dir
jemals ein Schmerz deutlicher wird in der Nähe des immer
trabenden Herzens, kommt das Brennen der Fußsohln
ihm, seinem Ursprung, zuvor mit ein paar dir
rasch in die Augen gejagten leiblichen Tränen.
Und dennoch, blindlings,
das Lächeln . . . . .

Engel! o nimms, pflücks, das kleinblütige Heilkraut.
Schaff eine Vase, verwahrs! Stells unter jene, uns n o c h nicht   60
offenen Freuden; in lieblicher Urne
rühms mit blumiger schwungiger Aufschrift:
                         „Subrisio Saltat.".

Du dann, Liebliche,
du, von den reizendsten Freuden
stumm Übersprungne. Vielleicht sind
deine Fransen glücklich für dich—,
oder über den jungen
prallen Brüsten die grüne metallene Seide
fühlt sich unendlich verwöhnt und entbehrt nichts.
Du   70
immerfort anders auf alle des Gleichgewichts schwankende Waagen
hingelegte Marktfrucht des Gleichmuts,
öffentlich unter den Schultern.

Wo, o wo ist der Ort,—ich trag ihn im Herzen—,
wo sie noch lange nicht k o n n t e n, noch von einander
abfieln, wie sich bespringende, nicht recht
paarige Tiere;—
wo die Gewichte noch schwer sind;
wo noch von ihren vergeblich   80

hardly attempted look . . . And again
that man is clapping his hands for the downward spring, and before
a single pain has got within range of your ever-
galloping heart, comes the tingling
in the soles of your feet, ahead of the spring that it springs from,
chasing into your eyes a few physical tears.
And, spite of all, blindly,
your smile. . . .

Angel! Oh, take it, pluck it, that small-flowered herb of healing!
Shape a vase to preserve it. Set it among those joys   60
not *yet* open to us; in a graceful urn
praise it, with florally-soaring inscription:
                                    "Subrisio Saltat.".

Then you, my darling,
mutely elided
by all the most exquisite joys. Perhaps
your frills are happy on your behalf,—
or over your tight young breasts
the green metallic silk
feels itself endlessly spoilt and in need of nothing.   70
You,
time after time, upon all of the quivering scale-pans of balance
freshly laid fruit of serenity,
publicly shown among shoulders.

Where, oh where in the world is that place in my heart
where they still were far from being *able*, still fell away
from each other like mounting animals, not yet
properly paired;—
where weights are still heavy,
and hoops still stagger   80

wirbelnden Stäben die Teller
torkeln. . . . .

Und plötzlich in diesem mühsamen Nirgends, plötzlich
die unsägliche Stelle, wo sich das reine Zuwenig
unbegreiflich verwandelt—, umspringt
in jenes leere Zuviel.
Wo die vielstellige Rechnung
zahlenlos aufgeht.

Plätze, o Platz in Paris, unendlicher Schauplatz,
wo die Modistin, Madame Lamort,   90
die ruhlosen Wege der Erde, endlose Bänder,
schlingt und windet und neue aus ihnen
Schleifen erfindet, Rüschen, Blumen, Kokarden, künstliche Früchte—, alle
unwahr gefärbt,—für die billigen
Winterhüte des Schicksals.

. . . .

Engel: es wäre ein Platz, den wir nicht wissen, und dorten,
auf unsäglichem Teppich, zeigten die Liebenden, die's hier
bis zum Können nie bringen, ihre kühnen
hohen Figuren des Herzschwungs,
ihre Türme aus Lust, ihre   100
längst, wo Boden nie war, nur aneinander
lehnenden Leitern, bebend,—und k ö n n t e n s,
vor den Zuschauern rings, unzähligen lautlosen Toten:
Würfen die dann ihre letzten, immer ersparten,
immer verborgenen, die wir nicht kennen, ewig
gültigen Münzen des Glücks vor das endlich
wahrhaft lächelnde Paar auf gestilltem
Teppich?

away from their vainly
twirling sticks?. . . . .

And then, in this wearisome nowhere, all of a sudden,
the ineffable spot where the pure too-little
incomprehensibly changes,—springs round
into that empty too-much?
Where the many-digited sum
solves into zero?

Squares, o square in Paris, infinite show-place,
where the modiste Madame Lamort   90
winds and binds the restless ways of the world,
those endless ribbons, to ever-new
creations of bow, frill, flower, cockade and fruit,
all falsely-coloured, to deck
the cheap winter-hats of Fate.

. . . .

Angel: suppose there's a place we know nothing about, and there,
on some indescribable carpet, lovers showed all that here
they're for ever unable to manage—their daring
lofty figures of heart-flight,
their towers of pleasure, their ladders,   100
long since, where ground never was, just quiveringly
propped by each other,—suppose they could manage it there,
before the spectators ringed round, the countless unmurmuring **dead:**
would not the dead then fling their last, their for ever reserved,
ever-concealed, unknown to us, ever-valid
coins of happiness down before the at last
truthfully smiling pair on the quietened
carpet?

Die Sechste Elegie

Feigenbaum, seit wie lange schon ists mir bedeutend,
    wie du die Blüte beinah ganz überschlägst
    und hinein in die zeitig entschlossene Frucht,
ungerühmt, drängst dein reines Geheimnis.
Wie der Fontäne Rohr treibt dein gebognes Gezweig
abwärts den Saft und hinan: und er springt aus dem Schlaf,
fast nicht erwachend, ins Glück seiner süßesten Leistung.
Sieh: wie der Gott in den Schwan.
                    . . . . . Wir aber verweilen,
ach, uns rühmt es zu blühn, und ins verspätete Innre
unserer endlichen Frucht gehn wir verraten hinein.
Wenigen steigt so stark der Andrang des Handelns,
daß sie schon anstehn und glühn in der Fülle des Herzens,
wenn die Verführung zum Blühn wie gelinderte Nachtluft
ihnen die Jugend des Munds, ihnen die Lider berührt:
Helden vielleicht und den frühe Hinüberbestimmten,
denen der gärtnernde Tod anders die Adern verbiegt.
Diese stürzen dahin: dem eigenen Lächeln
sind sie voran, wie das Rossegespann in den milden
muldigen Bildern von Karnak dem siegenden König.

Wunderlich nah ist der Held doch den jugendlich Toten. Dauern
ficht ihn nicht an. Sein Aufgang ist Dasein; beständig

The Sixth Elegy

FIG tree, how long it's been full meaning for me,
   the way you almost entirely omit to flower
   and into the seasonably-resolute fruit
uncelebratedly thrust your purest secret.
Like the tube of a fountain, your bent bough drives the sap
downwards and up: and it leaps from its sleep, scarce waking,
into the joy of its sweetest achievement. Look,
like Jupiter into the swan.

                        . . . . . But we, we linger,
alas, we glory in flowering; already betrayed
we reach the retarded core of our ultimate fruit.
In few the pressure of action rises so strongly
that already they're stationed and glowing in fulness of heart,
when, seductive as evening air, the temptation to flower,
touching the youth of their mouths, touching their eyelids, appears:
only in heroes, perhaps, and those marked for early removal,
those in whom gardening Death's differently twisted the veins.
These go plunging ahead: preceding their own
victorious smile, as the team of horse in the mildly-
moulded reliefs of Karnak the conquering King.

Yes, the Hero's strangely akin to the youthfully-dead. Continuance
doesn't concern him. His rising's existence. Time and again

nimmt er sich fort und tritt ins veränderte Sternbild
seiner steten Gefahr. Dort fänden ihn wenige. Aber,
das uns finster verschweigt, das plötzlich begeisterte Schicksal
singt ihn hinein in den Sturm seiner aufrauschenden Welt.
Hör ich doch keinen wie ihn. Auf einmal durchgeht mich
mit der strömenden Luft sein verdunkelter Ton.

Dann, wie verbärg ich mich gern vor der Sehnsucht: O wär ich,
wär ich ein Knabe und dürft es noch werden und säße   30
in die künftigen Arme gestützt und läse von Simson,
wie seine Mutter erst nichts und dann alles gebar.

War er nicht Held, schon in dir, o Mutter, begann nicht
dort schon, in dir, seine herrische Auswahl?
Tausende brauten im Schooß und wollten e r sein,
aber sieh: er ergriff und ließ aus, wählte und konnte.
Und wenn er Säulen zerstieß, so wars, da er ausbrach
aus der Welt deines Leibs in die engere Welt, wo er weiter
wählte und konnte. O Mütter der Helden,
o Ursprung reißender Ströme! Ihr Schluchten, in die sich   40
hoch von dem Herzrand, klagend,
schon die Mädchen gestürzt, künftig die Opfer dem Sohn.
Denn hinstürmte der Held durch Aufenthalte der Liebe,
jeder hob ihn hinaus, jeder ihn meinende Herzschlag,
abgewendet schon, stand er am Ende der Lächeln, anders.

he takes himself off and enters the changed constellation
his changeless peril's assumed. There few could find him. But Fate,
who deals so darkly with us, enraptured all of a sudden,
sings him into the storm of her roaring world.
None do I hear like him. There suddenly rushes through me,
borne by the streaming air, his dull-thunderous tone.

And then how gladly I'd hide from the longing: oh would,
would that I were a boy and might come to it yet, and be sitting,   30
propped upon arms still to be, and reading of Samson,
how his mother at first bore nothing, and, afterwards, all.

Was he not hero already, within you, O mother, and did not
his lordly choice begin there, already, within you?
Thousands were brewing in the womb and trying to be *he,*
but, look! he seized and discarded, chose and was able to do.
And if ever he shattered columns, that was the time, when he burst
out of the world of your body into the narrower world,
where he went on choosing and doing. O mothers of heroes!
Sources of ravaging rivers! Gorges wherein,   40
from high on the heart's edge, weeping,
maids have already plunged, victims—to be for the son.
For whenever the Hero stormed through the halts of love,
each heart beating for him could only lift him beyond it:
turning away, he'd stand at the end of the smiles—another.

Die Siebente Elegie

WERBUNG nicht mehr, nicht Werbung, entwachsene Stimme,
sei deines Schreies Natur; zwar schrieest du rein wie der Vogel,
wenn ihn die Jahreszeit aufhebt, die steigende, beinah verges-
send,
daß er ein kümmerndes Tier und nicht nur ein einzelnes Herz sei,
das sie ins Heitere wirft, in die innigen Himmel. Wie er, so
würbest du wohl, nicht minder—, daß, noch unsichtbar,
dich die Freundin erführ, die stille, in der eine Antwort
langsam erwacht und über dem Hören sich anwärmt,—
deinem erkühnten Gefühl die erglühte Gefühlin.
O und der Frühling begriffe—, da ist keine Stelle,   10
die nicht trüge den Ton Verkündigung. Erst jenen kleinen
fragenden Auflaut, den mit steigernder Stille
weithin umschweigt ein reiner bejahender Tag.
Dann die Stufen hinan, Ruf-Stufen hinan zum geträumten
Tempel der Zukunft—; dann den Triller, Fontäne,
die zu dem drängenden Strahl schon das Fallen zuvornimmt
im versprechlichen Spiel . . . Und vor sich, den Sommer.
Nicht nur die Morgen alle des Sommers—, nicht nur
wie sie sich wandeln in Tag und strahlen vor Anfang.
Nicht nur die Tage, die zart sind um Blumen, und oben,   20
um die gestalteten Bäume, stark und gewaltig.
Nicht nur die Andacht dieser entfalteten Kräfte,

The Seventh Elegy

Nor wooing, no longer shall wooing, voice that's outgrown it,
   be now the form of your cry; though you cried as pure as the bird
   when the surging season uplifts him, almost forgetting
he's merely a fretful creature and not just a single heart
she's tossing to brightness, to intimate azure. No less
than he, you, too, would be wooing some silent companion
to feel you, as yet unseen, some mate in whom a reply
was slowly awaking and warming itself as she listened,—
your own emboldened feeling's glowing fellow-feeling.
Oh, and Spring would understand—not a nook would fail   10
to re-echo annunciation. Re-echoing first the tiny
questioning pipe a purely affirmative day
quietly invests all round with magnifying stillness.
Then the long flight of steps, the call-steps, up to the dreamt-of
temple of what's to come;—then the trill, that fountain
caught as it rises by falling, in promiseful play,
for another thrusting jet . . . And before it, the Summer!
Not only all the summer dawns, not only
the way they turn into day and shine before sunrise.
Not only the days, so gentle round flowers, and, above,   20
around the configured trees, so mighty and strong.
Not only the fervour of these unfolded forces,

nicht nur die Wege, nicht nur die Wiesen im Abend,
nicht nur, nach spätem Gewitter, das atmende Klarsein,
nicht nur der nahende Schlaf und ein Ahnen, abends . . .
sondern die Nächte! Sondern die hohen, des Sommers,
Nächte, sondern die Sterne, die Sterne der Erde.
O einst tot sein und sie wissen unendlich,
alle die Sterne: denn wie, wie, wie sie vergessen!

Siehe, da rief ich die Liebende. Aber nicht s i e nur   30
käme . . . Es kämen aus schwächlichen Gräbern
Mädchen und ständen . . . Denn, wie beschränk ich,
wie, den gerufenen Ruf? Die Versunkenen suchen
immer noch Erde.—Ihr Kinder, ein hiesig
einmal ergriffenes Ding gälte für viele.
Glaubt nicht, Schicksal sei mehr als das Dichte der Kindheit;
wie überholtet ihr oft den Geliebten, atmend,
atmend nach seligem Lauf, auf nichts zu, ins Freie.
Hiersein ist herrlich. Ihr wußtet es, Mädchen, ihr auch,
die ihr scheinbar entbehrtet, versankt—, ihr, in den ärgsten   40
Gassen der Städte, Schwärende, oder dem Abfall
offene. Denn eine Stunde war jeder, vielleicht nicht
ganz eine Stunde, ein mit den Maßen der Zeit kaum
Meßliches zwischen zwei Weilen, da sie ein Dasein
hatte. Alles. Die Adern voll Dasein.
Nur, wir vergessen so leicht, was der lachende Nachbar
uns nicht bestätigt oder beneidet. Sichtbar
wollen wirs heben, wo doch das sichtbarste Glück uns
erst zu erkennen sich gibt, wenn wir es innen verwandeln.

Nirgends, Geliebte, wird Welt sein, als innen. Unser   50
Leben geht hin mit Verwandlung. Und immer geringer
schwindet das Außen. Wo einmal ein dauerndes Haus war,
schlägt sich erdachtes Gebild vor, quer, zu Erdenklichem
völlig gehörig, als ständ es noch ganz im Gehirne.

not only the walks, not only the evening meadows,
not only, after late thunder, the breathing clearness,
not only, with evening, sleep coming, and something surmised . . .
No, but the nights as well! the lofty, the summer
nights,—but the stars as well, the stars of the earth!
Oh, to be dead at last and endlessly know them,
all the stars! For how, how, how to forget them!

Look, I've been calling the lover. But not only she   30
would come . . . Out of unwithholding graves
girls would come and gather . . . For how could I limit
the call I had called? The sunken are always seeking
earth again.—You children, I'd say, a single
thing comprehended here's as good as a thousand.
Don't think Destiny's more than what's packed into childhood.
How often you'd overtake the beloved, panting,
panting for blissful career, without end, into freedom!
Life here's glorious! Even you knew it, you girls,
who went without, as it seemed, sank under,—you, in the vilest   40
streets of cities, festering, or open for refuse.
For to each was granted an hour,—perhaps not quite
so much as an hour—some span that could scarcely be measured
by measures of time, in between two whiles, when she really
possessed an existence. All. Veins full of existence.
But we so lightly forget what our laughing neighbour
neither confirms nor envies. We want to be visibly
able to show it, whereas the most visible joy
can only reveal itself to us when we've transformed it, within.

Nowhere, beloved, can world exist but within.   50
Life passes in transformation. And, ever diminishing,
vanishes what's outside. Where once was a lasting house,
up starts some invented structure across our vision, as fully
at home among concepts as though it still stood in a brain.

Weite Speicher der Kraft schafft sich der Zeitgeist, gestaltlos
wie der spannende Drang, den er aus allem gewinnt.
Tempel kennt er nicht mehr. Diese, des Herzens, Verschwendung
sparen wir heimlicher ein. Ja, wo noch eins übersteht,
ein einst gebetetes Ding, ein gedientes, geknietes—,
hält es sich, so wie es ist, schon ins Unsichtbare hin.   60
Viele gewahrens nicht mehr, doch ohne den Vorteil,
daß sie's nun i n n e r l i c h baun, mit Pfeilern und Statuen, größer!

Jede dumpfe Umkehr der Welt hat solche Enterbte,
denen das Frühere nicht und noch nicht das Nächste gehört.
Denn auch das Nächste ist weit für die Menschen. Uns soll
dies nicht verwirren; es stärke in uns die Bewahrung
der noch erkannten Gestalt. Dies s t a n d einmal unter Menschen,
mitten im Schicksal stands, im vernichtenden, mitten
im Nichtwissen-Wohin stand es, wie seiend, und bog
Sterne zu sich aus gesicherten Himmeln. Engel,   70
dir noch zeig ich es, d a ! in deinem Anschaun
steh es gerettet zuletzt, nun endlich aufrecht.
Säulen, Pylone, der Sphinx, das strebende Stemmen,
grau aus vergehender Stadt oder aus fremder, des Doms.
War es nicht Wunder? O staune, Engel, denn w i r sinds,
wir, o du Großer, erzähls, daß wir solches vermochten, mein Atem
reicht für die Rühmung nicht aus. So haben wir dennoch
nicht die Räume versäumt, diese gewährenden, diese
u n s e r e n Räume. (Was müssen sie fürchterlich groß sein,
da sie Jahrtausende nicht unseres Fühlns überfülln.)   80
Aber ein Turm war groß, nicht wahr? O Engel, er war es,—
groß, auch noch neben dir? Chartres war groß—und Musik
reichte noch weiter hinan und überstieg uns. Doch selbst nur
eine Liebende, oh, allein am nächtlichen Fenster. . . .
reichte sie dir nicht ans Knie—?

                      Glaub n i c h t, daß ich werbe.
Engel, und würb ich dich auch! Du kommst nicht. Denn mein

Spacious garners of power are formed by the Time Spirit, formless
as that tense urge he's extracting from everything else.
Temples he knows no longer. We're now more secretly saving
such lavish expenses of heart. Nay, even where one survives,
one single thing once prayed or tended or knelt to,
it's reaching, just as it is, into the unseen world.   60
Many perceive it no more, but neglect the advantage
of building it grandlier now, with pillars and statues, *within!*

Each torpid turn of the world has such disinherited children,
to whom no longer what's been, and not yet what's coming, belongs.
For the nearest, next coming, is remote for mankind. Though this
shall not confuse us, shall rather confirm us in keeping
still recognisable form. This *stood* once among mankind,
stood in the midst of Fate, the extinguisher, stood
in the midst of not-knowing-whither, as though it existed, and bowed
stars from established heavens towards it. Angel,   70
I'll show it to you as well—there! In your gaze
it shall stand redeemed at last, in a final uprightness.
Pillars, pylons, the Sphinx, all the striving thrust,
grey, from fading or foreign town, of the spire!
Wasn't all this a miracle? Angel, gaze, for it's *we*—
O mightiness, tell them that *we* were capable of it—my breath's
too short for this celebration. So, after all, we have *not*
failed to make use of the spaces, these generous spaces, these,
our spaces. (How terribly big they must be,
when, with thousands of years of our feeling, they're not over-crowded.) 80
But a tower was great, was it not? Oh, Angel, it was, though,—
even compared with you? Chartres was great—and music
towered still higher and passed beyond us. Why, even
a girl in love, alone, at her window, at night . . .
did she not reach to your knee?
                                    Don't think that I'm wooing!
Angel, even if I were, you'd never come. For my call

Anruf ist immer voll Hinweg; wider so starke
Strömung kannst du nicht schreiten. Wie ein gestreckter
Arm ist mein Rufen. Und seine zum Greifen
oben offene Hand bleibt vor dir
offen, wie Abwehr und Warnung,
Unfaßlicher, weitauf.

is always full of 'Away!' Against such a powerful
current you cannot advance. Like an outstretched
arm is my call. And its clutching, upwardly 90
open hand is always before you
as open for warding and warning,
aloft there, Inapprehensible.

Die Achte Elegie

Rudolf Kassner zugeeignet

Mit allen Augen sieht die Kreatur
das Offene. Nur unsre Augen sind
wie umgekehrt und ganz um sie gestellt
als Fallen, rings um ihren freien Ausgang.
Was draußen i s t , wir wissens aus des Tiers
Antlitz allein; denn schon das frühe Kind
wenden wir um und zwingens, daß es rückwärts
Gestaltung sehe, nicht das Offne, das
im Tiergesicht so tief ist. Frei von Tod.
I h n sehen wir allein; das freie Tier
hat seinen Untergang stets hinter sich
und vor sich Gott, und wenn es geht, so gehts
in Ewigkeit, so wie die Brunnen gehen.
Wir haben nie, nicht einen einzigen Tag,
den reinen Raum vor uns, in den die Blumen
unendlich aufgehn. Immer ist es Welt
und niemals Nirgends ohne Nicht:
das Reine, Unüberwachte, das man atmet und
unendlich w e i ß und nicht begehrt. Als Kind
verliert sich eins im Stilln an dies und wird
gerüttelt. Oder jener stirbt und i s t s.

The Eighth Elegy

Dedicated to Rudolf Kassner

W ITH all its eyes the creature-world beholds
the open. But our eyes, as though reversed,
encircle it on every side, like traps
set round its unobstructed path to freedom.
What *is* outside, we know from the brute's face
alone; for while a child's quite small we take it
and turn it round and force it to look backwards
at conformation, not that openness
so deep within the brute's face. Free from death.
We only see death; the free animal   10
has its decease perpetually behind it
and God in front, and when it moves, it moves
into eternity, like running springs.
We've never, no, not for a single day,
pure space before us, such as that which flowers
endlessly open into: always world,
and never nowhere without no: that pure,
unsuperintended element one breathes,
endlessly knows, and never craves. A child
sometimes gets quietly lost there, to be always   20
jogged back again. Or someone dies and *is* it.

Denn nah am Tod sieht man den Tod nicht mehr
und starrt h i n a u s, vielleicht mit großem Tierblick.
Liebende, wäre nicht der andre, der
die Sicht verstellt, sind nah daran und staunen . . .
Wie aus Versehn ist ihnen aufgetan
hinter dem andern . . . Aber über ihn
kommt keiner fort, und wieder wird ihm Welt.
Der Schöpfung immer zugewendet, sehn
wir nur auf ihr die Spiegelung des Frein,   30
von uns verdunkelt. Oder daß ein Tier,
ein stummes, aufschaut, ruhig durch uns durch.
Dieses heißt Schicksal: gegenüber sein
und nichts als das und immer gegenüber.

Wäre Bewußtheit unsrer Art in dem
sicheren Tier, das uns entgegenzieht
in anderer Richtung—, riß es uns herum
mit seinem Wandel. Doch sein Sein ist ihm
unendlich, ungefaßt und ohne Blick
auf seinen Zustand, rein, so wie sein Ausblick.   40
Und wo wir Zukunft sehn, dort sieht es Alles
und sich in Allem und geheilt für immer.

Und doch ist in dem wachsam warmen Tier
Gewicht und Sorge einer großen Schwermut.
Denn ihm auch haftet immer an, was uns
oft überwältigt,—die Erinnerung,
als sei schon einmal das, wonach man drängt,
näher gewesen, treuer und sein Anschluß
unendlich zärtlich. Hier ist alles Abstand,
und dort wars Atem. Nach der ersten Heimat   50
ist ihm die zweite zwitterig und windig.
O Seligkeit der k l e i n e n Kreatur,
die immer b l e i b t im Schooße, der sie austrug;

For, nearing death, one perceives death no longer,
and stares ahead—perhaps with large brute gaze.
Lovers—were not the other present, always
spoiling the view!—draw near to it and wonder. . . .
Behind the other, as though through oversight,
the thing's revealed . . . But no one gets beyond
the other, and so world returns once more.
Always facing Creation, we perceive there
only a mirroring of the free and open,   30
dimmed by our breath. Or that a dumb brute's calmly
raising its head to look us through and through.
That's what Destiny means: being opposite,
and nothing else, and always opposite.

Did consciousness such as we have exist
in the sure animal that moves towards us
upon a different course, the brute would drag us
round in its wake. But its own being for it
is infinite, inapprehensible,
unintrospective, pure, like its outward gaze.   40
Where we see Future, it sees Everything,
itself in Everything, for ever healed.

And yet, within the wakefully-warm beast
there lies the weight and care of a great sadness.
For that which often overwhelms us clings
to him as well,—a kind of memory
that what we're pressing after now was once
nearer and truer and attached to us
with infinite tenderness. Here all is distance,
there it was breath. Compared with that first home   50
the second seems ambiguous and draughty.
Oh bliss of *tiny* creatures that *remain*
for ever in the womb that brought them forth!

o Glück der Mücke, die noch i n n e n hüpft,
selbst wenn sie Hochzeit hat: denn Schooß ist Alles.
Und sieh die halbe Sicherheit des Vogels,
der beinah beides weiß aus seinem Ursprung,
als wär er eine Seele der Etrusker,
aus einem Toten, den ein Raum empfing,
doch mit der ruhenden Figur als Deckel.
Und wie bestürzt ist eins, das fliegen muß
und stammt aus einem Schooß. Wie vor sich selbst
erschreckt, durchzuckts die Luft, wie wenn ein Sprung
durch eine Tasse geht. So reißt die Spur
der Fledermaus durchs Porzellan des Abends.

Und wir: Zuschauer, immer, überall,
dem allen zugewandt und nie hinaus!
Uns überfüllts. Wir ordnens. Es zerfällt.
Wir ordnens wieder und zerfallen selbst.

Wer hat uns also umgedreht, daß wir,
was wir auch tun, in jener Haltung sind
von einem, welcher fortgeht? Wie er auf
dem letzten Hügel, der ihm ganz sein Tal
noch einmal zeigt, sich wendet, anhält, weilt—,
so leben wir und nehmen immer Abschied.

Joy of the gnat, that can still leap *within,*
even on its wedding-day: for womb is all.
Look at the half-assurance of the bird,
through origin almost aware of both,
like one of those Etruscan souls, escaped
from a dead man enclosed within a space
on which his resting figure forms a lid.   60
And how dismayed is any womb-born thing
that has to fly! As though it were afraid
of its own self, it zigzags through the air
like crack through cup. The way the track of a bat
goes rending through the evening's porcelain.

And we, spectators always, everywhere,
looking at, never out of, everything!
It fills us. We arrange it. It decays.
We re-arrange it, and decay ourselves.

Who's turned us round like this, so that we always,   70
do what we may, retain the attitude
of someone who's departing? Just as he,
on the last hill, that shows him all his valley
for the last time, will turn and stop and linger,
we live our lives, for ever taking leave.

Die Neunte Elegie

WARUM, wenn es angeht, also die Frist des Daseins
hinzubringen, als Lorbeer, ein wenig dunkler als alles
andere Grün, mit kleinen Wellen an jedem
Blattrand (wie eines Windes Lächeln)—: warum dann
Menschliches müssen—und, Schicksal vermeidend,
sich sehnen nach Schicksal? . . .

       Oh, nicht, weil Glück i s t,
dieser voreilige Vorteil eines nahen Verlusts.
Nicht aus Neugier, oder zur Übung des Herzens,
das auch im Lorbeer w ä r e . . . . .
Aber weil Hiersein viel ist, und weil uns scheinbar
alles das Hiesige braucht, dieses Schwindende, das
seltsam uns angeht. Uns, die Schwindendsten. Ein mal
jedes, nur ein mal. Ein mal und nichtmehr. Und wir auch
ein mal. Nie wieder. Aber dieses
ein mal gewesen zu sein, wenn auch nur ein mal:
i r d i s c h gewesen zu sein, scheint nicht widerrufbar.

Und so drängen wir uns und wollen es leisten,
wollens enthalten in unseren einfachen Händen,
im überfüllteren Blick und im sprachlosen Herzen.
Wollen es werden. Wem es geben? Am liebsten
alles behalten für immer . . . Ach, in den andern Bezug,

The Ninth Elegy

WHY, when this span of life might be fleeted away
as laurel, a little darker than all
the surrounding green, with tiny waves on the border
of every leaf (like the smile of a wind):—oh, why
have to be human, and, shunning Destiny,
long for Destiny? . . .
                              Not because happiness really
exists, that premature profit of imminent loss.
Not out of curiosity, not just to practise the heart,
that could still be there in laurel.   10
But because being here amounts to so much, because all
this Here and Now, so fleeting, seems to require us and strangely
concerns us. Us the most fleeting of all. Just once,
everything, only for once. Once and no more. And we, too,
once. And never again. But this
having been once, though only once,
having been once on earth—can it ever be cancelled?

And so we keep pressing on and trying to perform it,
trying to contain it within our simple hands,
in the more and more crowded gaze, in the speechless heart.   20
Trying to become it. To give it to whom? We'd rather
hold on to it all for ever. . . . Alas, but the other relation,—

wehe, was nimmt man hinüber? Nicht das Anschaun, das hier
langsam erlernte, und kein hier Ereignetes. Keins.
Also die Schmerzen. Also vor allem das Schwersein,
also der Liebe lange Erfahrung,—also
lauter Unsägliches. Aber später,
unter den Sternen, was solls: d i e sind b e s s e r unsäglich.
Bringt doch der Wanderer auch vom Hange des Bergrands
nicht eine Hand voll Erde ins Tal, die allen unsägliche, sondern   30
ein erworbenes Wort, reines, den gelben und blaun
Enzian. Sind wir vielleicht h i e r , um zu sagen: Haus,
Brücke, Brunnen, Tor, Krug, Obstbaum, Fenster,—
höchstens: Säule, Turm . . . aber zu s a g e n, verstehs,
oh zu sagen s o, wie selber die Dinge niemals
innig meinten zu sein. Ist nicht die heimliche List
dieser verschwiegenen Erde, wenn sie die Liebenden drängt,
daß sich in ihrem Gefühl jedes und jedes entzückt?
Schwelle: was ists für zwei
Liebende, daß sie die eigne ältere Schwelle der Tür   40
ein wenig verbrauchen, auch sie, nach den vielen vorher
und vor den Künftigen . . . , leicht.

H i e r ist des S ä g l i c h e n Zeit, h i e r seine Heimat.
Sprich und bekenn. Mehr als je
fallen die Dinge dahin, die erlebbaren, denn,
was sie verdrängend ersetzt, ist ein Tun ohne Bild.
Tun unter Krusten, die willig zerspringen, sobald
innen das Handeln entwächst und sich anders begrenzt.
Zwischen den Hämmern besteht
unser Herz, wie die Zunge   50
zwischen den Zähnen, die doch,
dennoch die preisende bleibt.

Preise dem Engel die Welt, nicht die unsägliche, ihm
kannst du nicht großtun mit herrlich Erfühltem; im Weltall,

what can be taken across? Not the art of seeing, learnt here
so slowly, and nothing that's happened here. Nothing at all.
Sufferings, then. Above all, the hardness cf life,
the long experience of love; in fact,
purely untellable things. But later,
under the stars, what then? the more deeply untellable stars?
For the wanderer doesn't bring from the mountain slope
a handful of earth to the valley, untellable earth, but only   30
some word he has won, a pure word, the yellow and blue
gentian. Are we, perhaps, here just for saying: House,
Bridge, Fountain, Gate, Jug, Olive tree, Window,—
possibly: Pillar, Tower? . . . . but for saying, remember,
oh, for such saying as never the things themselves
hoped so intensely to be. Is not the secret purpose
of this sly earth, in urging a pair of lovers,
just to make everything leap with ecstasy in them?
Threshold: how much it can mean
to two lovers, that they should be wearing their own   40
worn threshold a little, they too, after the many before,
before the many to come, ... as a matter of course!

Here is the time for the Tellable, *here* is its home.
Speak and proclaim. More than ever
the things we can live with are falling away, and their place
being oustingly taken up by an imageless act.
Act under crusts, that will readily split as soon
as the doing within outgrows them and takes a new outline.
Between the hammers lives on
our heart, as between the teeth   50
the tongue, which, nevertheless,
remains the bestower of praise.

Praise the world to the Angel, not the untellable: you
can't impress him with the splendour you've felt; in the cosmos

wo er fühlender fühlt, bist du ein Neuling. Drum zeig
ihm das Einfache, das, von Geschlecht zu Geschlechtern gestaltet,
als ein Unsriges lebt neben der Hand und im Blick.
Sag ihm die Dinge. Er wird staunender stehn; wie du standest
bei dem Seiler in Rom, oder beim Töpfer am Nil.
Zeig ihm, wie glücklich ein Ding sein kann, wie schuldlos und unser,   60
wie selbst das klagende Leid rein zur Gestalt sich entschließt,
dient als ein Ding, oder stirbt in ein Ding—, und jenseits
selig der Geige entgeht. Und diese, von Hingang
lebenden Dinge verstehn, daß du sie rühmst; vergänglich,
traun sie ein Rettendes uns, den Vergänglichsten, zu.
Wollen, wir sollen sie ganz im unsichtbarn Herzen verwandeln
in—o unendlich—in uns! wer wir am Ende auch seien.

Erde, ist es nicht dies, was du willst: u n s i c h t b a r
in uns erstehn?—Ist es dein Traum nicht,
einmal unsichtbar zu sein?—Erde! unsichtbar!   70
Was, wenn Verwandlung nicht, ist dein drängender Auftrag?
Erde, du liebe, ich will. Oh glaub, es bedürfte
nicht deiner Frühlinge mehr, mich dir zu gewinnen, einer,
ach, ein einziger ist schon dem Blute zu viel.
Namenlos bin ich zu dir entschlossen, von weit her.
Immer warst du im Recht, und dein heiliger Einfall
ist der vertrauliche Tod.
Siehe, ich lebe. Woraus? Weder Kindheit noch Zukunft
werden weniger . . . . . Überzähliges Dasein
entspringt mir im Herzen.   80

where he more feelingly feels you're only a tyro. So show him
some simple thing, remoulded by age after age,
till it lives in our hands and eyes as a part of ourselves.
Tell him *things*. He'll stand more astonished; as you did
beside the roper in Rome or the potter in Egypt.
Show him how happy a thing can be, how guileless and ours;   60
how even the moaning of grief purely determines on form,
serves as a thing, or dies into a thing,—to escape
to a bliss beyond the fiddle. These things that live on departure
understand when you praise them: fleeting, they look for
rescue through something in us, the most fleeting of all.
Want us to change them entirely, within our invisible hearts,
into—oh, endlessly—into ourselves! Whosoever we are.

Earth, isn't this what you want: an invisible
re-arising in us? Is it not your dream
to be one day invisible? Earth! invisible!   70
What is your urgent command, if not transformation?
Earth, you darling, I will! Oh, believe me, you need
your Springs no longer to win me: a single one,
just one, is already more than my blood can endure.
I've now been unspeakably yours for ages and ages.
You were always right, and your holiest inspiration's
Death, that friendly Death.
Look, I am living. On what? Neither childhood nor future
are growing less. . . . . Supernumerous existence
wells up in my heart.   80

Die Zehnte Elegie

Dass ich dereinst, an dem Ausgang der grimmigen Einsicht,
Jubel und Ruhm aufsinge zustimmenden Engeln.
Daß von den klargeschlagenen Hämmern des Herzens
keiner versage an weichen, zweifelnden oder
reißenden Saiten. Daß mich mein strömendes Antlitz
glänzender mache; daß das unscheinbare Weinen
blühe. O wie werdet ihr dann, Nächte, mir lieb sein,
gehärmte. Daß ich euch knieender nicht, untröstliche Schwestern,
hinnahm, nicht in euer gelöstes
Haar mich gelöster ergab. Wir, Vergeuder der Schmerzen.   10
Wie wir sie absehn voraus, in die traurige Dauer,
ob sie nicht enden vielleicht. Sie aber sind ja
unser winterwähriges Laub, unser dunkeles Sinngrün,
e i n e der Zeiten des heimlichen Jahres—, nicht nur
Zeit—, sind Stelle, Siedelung, Lager, Boden, Wohnort.

Freilich, wehe, wie fremd sind die Gassen der Leid-Stadt,
wo in der falschen, aus Übertönung gemachten
Stille, stark, aus der Gußform des Leeren der Ausguß,
prahlt der vergoldete Lärm, das platzende Denkmal.
O, wie spurlos zerträte ein Engel ihnen den Trostmarkt,   20
den die Kirche begrenzt, ihre fertig gekaufte:
reinlich und zu und enttäuscht wie ein Postamt am Sonntag.

The Tenth Elegy

SOMEDAY, emerging at last from this terrifying vision,
    may I burst into jubilant praise to assenting Angels!
    May not even one of the clear-struck keys of the heart
fail to respond through alighting on slack or doubtful
or rending strings! May a new-found splendour appear
in my streaming face! May inconspicuous Weeping
flower! How dear you will be to me then, you Nights
of Affliction! Oh, why did I not, inconsolable sisters,
more bendingly kneel to receive you, more loosely surrender
myself to your loosened hair? We wasters of sorrows!   10
How we stare away into sad endurance beyond them,
trying to foresee their end! Whereas they are nothing else
than our winter foliage, our sombre evergreen, *one*
of the seasons of our interior year,—not only
season—they're also place, settlement, camp, soil, dwelling.

Strange, though, alas! are the streets of the City of Pain,
where, in the seeming stillness of uproar outroared,
stoutly, a thing cast out from the mould of vacuity,
swaggers that gilded fuss, the bursting memorial.
How an Angel would tread beyond trace their market of comfort,   20
with the church alongside, bought ready for use: as clean
and disenchanted and shut as the Post on a Sunday!

Draußen aber kräuseln sich immer die Ränder von Jahrmarkt.
Schaukeln der Freiheit! Taucher und Gaukler des Eifers!
Und des behübschten Glücks figürliche Schießstatt,
wo es zappelt von Ziel und sich blechern benimmt,
wenn ein Geschickterer trifft. Von Beifall zu Zufall
taumelt er weiter; denn Buden jeglicher Neugier
werben, trommeln und plärrn. Für Erwachsene aber
ist noch besonders zu sehn, wie das Geld sich vermehrt, anatomisch,   30
nicht zur Belustigung nur: der Geschlechtsteil des Gelds,
alles, das Ganze, der Vorgang—, das unterrichtet und macht
fruchtbar . . . .
       . . . Oh aber gleich darüber hinaus,
hinter der letzten Planke, beklebt mit Plakaten des „Todlos",
jenes bitteren Biers, das den Trinkenden süß scheint,
wenn sie immer dazu frische Zerstreuungen kaun . . . ,
gleich im Rücken der Planke, gleich dahinter, ists w i r k l i c h.
Kinder spielen, und Liebende halten einander,—abseits,
ernst, im ärmlichen Gras, und Hunde haben Natur.
Weiter noch zieht es den Jüngling; vielleicht, daß er eine junge   40
Klage liebt . . . Hinter ihr her kommt er in Wiesen. Sie sagt:
Weit. Wir wohnen dort draußen. . . .
              Wo? Und der Jüngling
folgt. Ihn rührt ihre Haltung. Die Schulter, der Hals—, vielleicht
ist sie von herrlicher Herkunft. Aber er läßt sie, kehrt um,
wendet sich, winkt . . . Was solls? Sie ist eine Klage.

Nur die jungen Toten, im ersten Zustand
zeitlosen Gleichmuts, dem der Entwöhnung,
folgen ihr liebend. Mädchen
wartet sie ab und befreundet sie. Zeigt ihnen leise,   50
was sie an sich hat. Perlen des Leids und die feinen
Schleier der Duldung.—Mit Jünglingen geht sie
schweigend.

Outside, though, there's always the billowing edge of the fair.
Swings of Freedom! Divers and Jugglers of Zeal!
And the life-like shooting-ranges of bedizened Happiness: targets
tumbling in tinny contortions whenever some better shot
happens to hit one. Cheer-struck, on he goes reeling
after his luck. For booths that can please
the most curious tastes are drumming and bawling. Especially
worth seeing (for adults only): the breeding of Money!   30
Anatomy made amusing! Money's organs on view!
Nothing concealed! Instructive, and guaranteed
to increase fertility! . . . .
                    . . . Oh, and then just outside,
behind the last hoarding, plastered with placards for "Deathless,"
that bitter beer that tastes quite sweet to its drinkers
so long as they chew with it plenty of fresh distractions,—
just at the back of the hoardings, just behind them, it's real!
Children are playing, and lovers holding each other,—aside,
gravely, in pitiful grass, and dogs are following nature.   40
The youth is drawn further on; perhaps he's in love with a youthful
Lament . . . He emerges behind her into the meadows, she says:
A long way. We live out there. . . .
                         Where? And the youth
follows. He's touched by her manner. Her shoulder, her neck,—perhaps
she comes of a famous stock? But he leaves her, turns back,
looks round, nods . . . What's the use? She's just a Lament.

Only the youthfully-dead, in their first condition
of timeless serenity, that of being weaned,
follow her lovingly. Girls   50
she awaits and befriends. Gently, she shows them
what she is wearing. Pearls of Pain and the fine-spun
Veils of Patience.—Youths
she walks with in silence.

Aber dort, wo sie wohnen, im Tal, der Älteren eine, der Klagen
nimmt sich des Jünglinges an, wenn er fragt:—Wirwaren,
sagt sie, ein großes Geschlecht, einmal, wir Klagen. Die Väter
trieben den Bergbau dort in dem großen Gebirg; bei Menschen
findest du manchmal ein Stück geschliffenes Urleid
oder, aus altem Vulkan, schlackig versteinerten Zorn.   60
Ja, das stammte von dort. Einst waren wir reich.—

Und sie leitet ihn leicht durch die weite Landschaft der Klagen,
zeigt ihm die Säulen der Tempel oder die Trümmer
jener Burgen, von wo Klage-Fürsten das Land
einstens weise beherrscht. Zeigt ihm die hohen
Tränenbäume und Felder blühender Wehmut,
(Lebendige kennen sie nur als sanftes Blattwerk);
zeigt ihm die Tiere der Trauer, weidend,—und manchmal
schreckt ein Vogel und zieht, flach ihnen fliegend durchs Aufschaun,
weithin das schriftliche Bild seines vereinsamten Schreis.—   70
Abends führt sie ihn hin zu den Gräbern der Alten
aus dem Klage-Geschlecht, den Sibyllen und Warn-Herrn.
Naht aber Nacht, so wandeln sie leiser, und bald
mondets empor, das über alles
wachende Grab-Mal. Brüderlich jenem am Nil,
der erhabene Sphinx—: der verschwiegenen Kammer
Antlitz.
Und sie staunen dem krönlichen Haupt, das für immer,
schweigend, der Menschen Gesicht
auf die Waage der Sterne gelegt.   80

Nicht erfaßt es sein Blick, im Frühtod
schwindelnd. Aber ihr Schaun,
hinter dem Pschent-Rand hervor, scheucht es die Eule. Und sie,
streifend im langsamen Abstrich die Wange entlang,
jene der reifesten Rundung,
zeichnet weich in das neue

But there, where they live, in the valley, one of the elder Laments
takes to the youth when he questions her:—We were once,
she says, a great family, we Lamentations. Our fathers
worked the mines in that mountain-range: among men
you'll find a lump, now and then, of polished original pain,
or of drossy petrified rage from some old volcano.   60
Yes, that came from there. We used to be rich.

And lightly she leads him on through the spacious landscape
of Lamentation, shows him the temple columns, the ruins
of towers from which, long ago, Lords of the House of Lament
wisely governed the land. Shows him the tall
Tear trees, shows him the fields of flowering Sadness
(only as tender foliage known to the living);
shows him the pasturing herds of Grief,—and, at times,
a startled bird, flying straight through their field of vision,
scrawls the far-stretching screed of its lonely cry.—   70
At evening she leads him on to the graves of the longest
lived of the House of Lament, the sibyls and warners.
But, night approaching, they move more gently, and soon
upsurges, bathed in moonlight, the all-
guarding sepulchral stone. Twin-brother to that on the Nile,
the lofty Sphinx, the taciturn chamber's gaze.
And they start at the regal head that has silently poised,
for ever, the human face
on the scale of the stars.

His sight, still dizzy with early death,   80
can't take it in. But her gaze
frightens an owl from behind the pschent. And the bird,
brushing, in slow neat-quitting, along the cheek,
the one with the ripest curve,
faintly inscribes on the new

Totengehör, über ein doppelt
aufgeschlagenes Blatt, den unbeschreiblichen Umriß.

Und höher, die Sterne. Neue. Die Sterne des Leidlands.
Langsam nennt sie die Klage: „Hier,   90
siehe: den *Reiter,* den *Stab,* und das vollere Sternbild
nennen sie: *Fruchtkranz.* Dann, weiter, dem Pol zu:
Wiege, Weg, das brennende Buch, Puppe, Fenster.
Aber im südlichen Himmel, rein wie im Innern
einer gesegneten Hand, das klar erglänzende *M,*
das die Mütter bedeutet . . . . .“

Doch der Tote muß fort, und schweigend bringt ihn die ältere
Klage bis an die Talschlucht,
wo es schimmert im Mondschein:
die Quelle der Freude. In Ehrfurcht   100
nennt sie sie, sagt: „Bei den Menschen
ist sie ein tragender Strom.“

Stehn am Fuß des Gebirgs.
Und da umarmt sie ihn, weinend.

Einsam steigt er dahin, in die Berge des Urleids.
Und nicht einmal sein Schritt klingt aus dem tonlosen Los.

Aber erweckten sie uns, die unendlich Toten, ein Gleichnis,
siehe, sie zeigten vielleicht auf die Kätzchen der leeren
Hasel, die hängenden, oder
meinten den Regen, der fällt auf dunkles Erdreich im Frühjahr.—   110

Und wir, die an s t e i g e n d e s Glück
denken, empfänden die Rührung,
die uns beinah bestürzt,
wenn ein Glückliches f ä l l t.

death-born hearing, as though on the double
page of an opened book, the indescribable outline.

And, higher, the stars. New ones. Stars of the Land of Pain.
Slowly she names them: "There,
look: the *Rider*, the *Staff*, and that fuller constellation   90
they call *Fruitgarland*. Then, further, towards the Pole:
Cradle, Way, The Burning Book, Doll, Window.
But up in the southern sky, pure as within the palm
of a consecrated hand, the clearly-resplendent *M*,
standing for Mothers. . . . ."

But the dead must go on, and, in silence, the elder Lament
brings him as far as the gorge
where it gleams in the moonlight,—
there, the source of Joy. With awe
she names it, says "Among men   100
it's a carrying stream."

They stand at the foot of the range.
And there she embraces him, weeping.

Alone, he climbs to the mountains of Primal Pain.
And never once does his step resound from the soundless fate.

And yet, were they waking a likeness within us, the endlessly dead,
look, they'd be pointing, perhaps, to the catkins, hanging
from empty hazels, or else they'd be meaning the rain
that falls on the dark earth in the early Spring.

And we, who have always thought   110
of happiness climbing, would feel
the emotion that almost startles
when happiness falls.

Commentary

*T*HIS *Commentary has been made as brief as possible. The purpose of the analyses is to enable the reader to perceive at a glance what, roughly speaking, each* ELEGY *is 'about'; they should be regarded as scaffoldings, which may be discarded after they have served their purpose, and not as attempts to confine Rilke's statements, developments, and transitions within a rigid logical frame. Comments on particular passages have been made only where they seemed really necessary. Ultimately, each reader must be left to overcome the 'difficulties' of the* ELEGIES *for himself, and, to do this, it is better to work outwards, from central positions and general conceptions, than inwards, from particular passages whose precise interpretation is often a matter of dispute.*

The Angel

One must begin with some understanding of what Rilke meant by the Angels, those imaginary beings which dominate the first two *Elegies,* and which continually reappear in the later ones. In the letter to his Polish translator, he wrote:

The "Angel" of the Elegies has nothing to do with the Angel of the Christian heaven (rather with the angelic figures of Islam) . . . The Angel of the Elegies is the creature in whom that transformation of the visible into the invisible we are performing already appears complete . . . The Angel of the Elegies is the being who vouches for the recognition of a higher degree of reality in the invisible.—Therefore "terrible" to us, because we, its lovers and transformers, still depend on the visible. (Briefe aus Muzot, 337.)

The Angel may be described as the hypostatisation of the idea of a perfect consciousness—of a being in whom the limitations and contradictions of present human nature have been transcended, a being in whom thought and action, insight and achievement, will and capability, the actual and the ideal, are one. He is both an inspiration and a rebuke, a source of consolation and also a source of terror; for, while he guarantees the validity of Man's highest aspirations and gives what Rilke would call a "direction" to his heart, he is at the same time a perpetual reminder of man's immeasurable remoteness from his goal.

Angels had appeared in Rilke's poetry from the beginning, and it would be interesting to trace therein the development of these, as of other, symbols; the conception of the 'terrible' Angel, however, the Angel of the *Elegies,* seems to have been formed during the critical years, 1910–12. He felt that the completion of *Malte Laurids Brigge,* in 1910, marked the end of a period in his life, and that it would be impossible to go on writing as though nothing had happened. His letters during the next two or three years are full of questionings and speculations about the new beginning that must be made, the new road that must be taken. He often felt that what was required of him was, as it were, a return from the world of things to the world of people; but, after many self-reproaches for his incapacity to give to others according to what he felt he received from them, for his insufficiency in love, we find him writing, in 1913, to Karl von der Heydt:

It would be inconsistent with the passionateness of the Angels to be specta-tors; they surpass us in action precisely as much as God surpasses them. I regard them as the assailants par excellence, and you must defer to me here —I've given security: for when, on my return from a thorough immersion in things and animals, I was looking forward to a course in humanity, lo and behold! the next but one, angelity, was set before me: thus I've skipped people, and am now looking cordially back at them. (Briefe aus den Jahren 1907–1914, 275.) With which may be compared a passage from a letter written in 1915, quoted on page 10 of the Introduction: *This world, regarded no longer from the human point of view, but as it is within the angel, is perhaps my real task, one, at any rate, in which all my previous attempts would converge.*

In the *Elegies* the predominant symbol is the Angel, the superhuman, and the predominant theme is Lament (*Klage*)—lament over the limitations and deficiencies of human nature; in the *Sonnets to Orpheus* the predominant symbol is Orpheus, the ideal poet, the topmost branch of the human tree, and the predominant theme is Praise (*Rühmung*). There is Praise in some of the *Elegies* (notably in the *Ninth,* where it predominates), and there is Lament in some of the *Sonnets,* but, in the main, *Elegies* and *Sonnets* may be re-garded as the expressions of two distinguishable but inseparable *moments* in

Rilke's attitude to life, and each of these two works should be read and remembered in the light of the other.

The First Elegy

The ideal of complete and undivided consciousness, where will and capability, thought and action, vision and realisation are one, is the highest Man can form, and yet, so impossible is it for Man to realise this ideal, to become like the Angels, that it is rather a rebuke than an inspiration. What, then, remains for Man? Perhaps, in Pater's phrase, to give the highest possible significance to his moments as they pass; to be continually prepared for those moments when eternity is perceived behind the flux of time, those moments when

> *the light of sense*
> *goes out, but with a flash that has revealed*
> *the invisible world.*

But the price of these moments of insight is a constant attentiveness and loyalty to all things and relationships, even the humblest and least spectacular, that immediately surround us; and from this mission, or task, we are continually distracted by all kinds of imaginary possibilities—above all, by the illusory ideal of some permanently satisfying possession, and, in particular, by the longing for some ideal lover or companion. And yet, declares Rilke, the highest kind of love is that which is unrequited, which is content simply to endure and, thereby, to *become*. Let us, then, since the Angels are too immeasurably beyond us, take as our examples the great lovers, and, also, those who have died young, through reflexion on whose destiny we shall achieve an intuition, which will still more deeply reconcile us to the fact of our transitoriness, into the unity of life and death and the complementariness of sorrow and joy.

The main themes of the *Elegies* have now been stated: the contrast between the Angels and Man; the recognition of Man's transitoriness, and the suggestion that this limitation may also be the condition of a special kind of activity; the insistence on the destinies of the great lovers and of the early-departed, and, although he is only incidentally mentioned, of the Hero, as keys to the true meaning of life and death, or, rather, to their ultimate identity.

l. 17: *O, and there's Night, there's Night*
On what Night meant to Rilke, both literally and as a symbol for the

mysterious and the unknown, see the poems on Night in *Later Poems*, 109 ff., and the Commentary thereon.

l. 22: *Fling the emptiness out of your arms*
The emptiness caused by the absence of the longed-for and unknown beloved.

ll. 28–29:   *a violin*
            would be giving itself to someone
Cf. the poem *Der Nachbar* (*The Neighbour*) in the *Buch der Bilder* (*Gesammelte Werke*, II, 42):

> *Fremde Geige, gehst du mir nach?*
> *In wieviel fernen Städten schon sprach*
> *deine einsame Nacht zu meiner?*
> *Spielen dich Hunderte? Spielt dich einer?*
>
> *Gibt es in allen grossen Städten*
> *solche, die sich ohne dich*
> *schon in den Flüssen verloren hätten?*
> *Und warum trifft es immer mich?*
>
> *Warum bin ich immer der Nachbar derer,*
> *die dich bange zwingen zu singen*
> *und zu sagen: Das Leben ist schwerer*
> *als die Schwere von allen Dingen?*

> *Unknown violin, are you following me?*
> *In how many distant cities already*
> *has your lonely night spoken to mine?*
> *Are a hundred playing you? Is one?*
>
> *Are there in all great cities*
> *such as, without you, would long ago*
> *have lost themselves in the rivers?*
> *And why does it always come home to me?*
>
> *Why am I always the neighbour of those*
> *who timidly force you to sing*
> *and to say: Life is harder and heavier*
> *than the weight of everything else?*

ll. 31–32: *distracted by expectation, as though all this*
were announcing someone to love

In the letters written between 1910 and 1914, those restless years which followed the completion of *Malte Laurids Brigge*, we continually find Rilke expressing a longing for human companionship and affection, and then, often immediately afterwards, asking whether he could really respond to such companionship if it were offered to him, and wondering whether, after all, his real task may not lie elsewhere. This longing and this dividedness are most poignantly expressed in four of the *Later Poems* and in the various passages from his letters quoted in the Commentary thereon (97–100, 245–52). Here, two characteristic extracts must suffice. In October, 1913, he wrote to Lou Andreas-Salomé: *Will you believe me, when I tell you that the sight of a woman who passed me in a quiet street in Rouen so disturbed me, that thereafter I could see almost nothing, concentrate on nothing? . . .*

Reading something, resting, looking out—yes, I could be contented with everything, if only it were entirely mine again, and did not keep discharging itself into longing. I'm alarmed when I think of the way I've been living out of myself, as though always standing at a telescope, ascribing to every woman that approached a bliss that could certainly never have been discovered in one of them: my bliss, the bliss—once—of my loneliest hours. (*Briefe aus den Jahren 1907–1914*, 301–2.) Ten months earlier, he had written to Princess Marie, from Spain:

Alas! I have not yet quite got over expecting the "nouvelle opération" from some human hand; and yet why, since my destiny is, as it were, to pass by the human, to reach the uttermost, the edge of the earth, as recently in Cordova . . . (*Op. cit.*, 258.)

l. 35:   *sing the great lovers*
See Appendix I.

l. 40: *Consider: the Hero continues, even his fall*
was a pretext for further existence, an ultimate birth

The Hero does not require our praise, for his fame lives on among men, but the names of lovers are forgotten, as though Nature had not the power to preserve them in human memory, but took them back to herself.

l. 45: *Gaspara Stampa*
She was born in 1523, in Padua, of a noble Milanese family, by whom, as her contemporaries would have said, she was 'exquisitely' educated. In Venice, at the age of twenty-six, she fell desperately in love with the young Collaltino,

Count of Collalto and Lord of Treviso. After a few years of mutual happiness, he went to France to fight for Henry II, forgot her, and consoled himself with other beauties. When at last he returned, a kind of duty prevented him from openly breaking with the woman he no longer loved. At first she was full of happiness; then she began to learn the truth. He finally left her and married. She consoled herself partly with other lovers and partly with religion, and died in 1554, at the age of thirty-one. The whole story of her love for Collaltino is recorded in some two hundred sonnets, of which the following, which may be supposed to have appealed particularly to Rilke, is offered as an example:

Sonetto LXXXVIII

Ma che, sciocca, dich 'io? perchè vaneggio?
  Perchè sì fuggo questo chiaro inganno?
  Perchè sgravarmi da sì util danno,
  Pronta ne' danni miei, ad Amor chieggio?
Come fuor di me stessa non mi avvegio
  Che quante ebber mai gioie e quante avranno,
  Quante fur donne mai, quante saranno,
  Co' miei chiari martír passo e pareggio?
Chè l'arder per cagione alta e gentile
  Ogni aspra vita fa dolce e beata
  Più che gioir per cosa abbietta e vile.
Ed io ringrazio Amor che destinata
  M'abbia a tal foco, che da Battro a Tile
  Spero anche un giorno andar chiara e lodata.

But what, in my folly, am I saying? Why am I raving? Why do I so shun this splendid deception? Why, prompt in my own losses, do I beg love to disburden me from such profitable loss? Why, as though out of my senses, do I not perceive that as many joys as ever had or shall have as many ladies as ever were or will be, I, with my splendid torments, surpass and equal? For the ardour kindled by a lofty and gentle cause makes every sour life sweet, and more blessed than delight in something abject and vile. And I thank Love that he has destined me for such fire that I even hope one day to be renowned and praised from Battro to Tile.

l. 64:   *as, lately, the tablet in Santa Maria Formosa*
A famous church in Venice. Rilke was in Venice during March and April, 1911, and again, on a short visit from Duino, in November. This *Elegy* was written in the following January. In the periodical *Die Schildgenossen*

(XVII, 2) the distinguished Catholic theologian, Romano Guardini, writes:

When, a short time ago, I was in this church, which is distinguished from the other Venetian churches by its so clear and severe form, I looked for the tablet and found, near to the right side altar, the one Rilke may have had in mind. Its inscription reads:

VIXI ALIIS DUM VITA FUIT
POST FUNERA TANDEM
NON PERII AT GELIDO
IN MARMORE VIVO MIHI
HERMANUS GULIELMUS ERAM
ME FLANDRIA LUGET
HADRIA SUSPIRAT
PAUPERIESQ. VOCAT
OBIIT XVI KAL. OCTOB.
MDXCIII.

While life lasted I lived for others; now, after death, I have not perished, but in cold marble live for myself. I was Hermann Wilhelm. Flanders mourns for me, Adria sighs for me, poverty calls for me.

He died on the 16th of October, 1593.

It will be seen that the epitaph itself forms four elegiac lines.

ll. 66–67:   *that hinders*
       a little, at times, their purely-proceeding spirits

Hinders, that is to say, their gradual weaning from terrestrial things, their progress in eternity. The matter is regarded both subjectively and objectively, from our point of view and from theirs, for they are both 'somewhere else' and, also, in our hearts.

ll. 82–83:   *The eternal*
       torrent whirls all the ages through either realm

IN THE "ELEGIES," Rilke wrote to his Polish translator, AFFIRMATION OF LIFE *AND* AFFIRMATION OF DEATH REVEAL THEMSELVES AS ONE. *To concede the one without the other is, as is here experienced and celebrated, a restriction that finally excludes all infinity. Death is our reverted, our unilluminated,* SIDE OF LIFE: *we must try to achieve the greatest possible consciousness of our existence, which is at home in* BOTH OF THESE UNLIMITED PROVINCES, *which is* INEXHAUSTIBLY NOURISHED OUT OF BOTH . . . *The true form of life extends through* BOTH *regions, the blood of the mightiest circulation pulses through* BOTH: THERE IS NEITHER A HERE NOR A BEYOND, BUT ONLY THE GREAT UNITY, *in which the "Angels," those beings that surpass us, are at home.* (*Briefe aus Muzot*, 332–33.)

l. 90:   *the mourning for Linos*

Linos, whose legend has many forms and some resemblance to that of
Adonis, was originally, it would seem, a god of the old Greek nature-worship,
and the Linos-song (mentioned by Homer, *Iliad,* XVIII, 570) a dirge for the
departing summer. Sometimes the origin of song and music in general was
connected with his dirge, and it was said that those who had been benumbed
with fear and horror at his death were reawakened to life by the song of
Orpheus.

The Second Elegy

In the *First Elegy* affirmation, on the whole, predominates over negation,
and praise, or celebration, over lament. The limitations of Man have been
recognised, but it has been suggested that they may, perhaps, be the condi-
tions of a special kind of activity. Nevertheless, the value of an affirmation
depends on the weight of conquered negation behind it, and in the succeeding
Elegies it is negation that predominates, insistence on the limitations of Man.

If a way to the better there be, it exacts a full look at the worst:

This 'look at the worst' Rilke now proceeds to take, and descends, like Or-
pheus, to sound his lyre among the shadows. In the *Second Elegy* he insists
on the contrast between the complete and continuous self-awareness of the
Angels and the fragmentary and intermittent self-awareness of Man: not
only the whole of his life on earth, but his very identity from moment to
moment is as a vapour that vanisheth away. Ordinary lovers, however it may
be with those rare spirits celebrated in the *First Elegy,* seem to obtain no
more than a fleeting intuition of eternity behind the flux of time. 'Our heart
transcends us,' our reach so greatly exceeds our grasp, that we had better,
perhaps, content ourselves with a kind of sad moderation, a μηδὲν ἄγαν,
neither asking nor giving too much. Rilke recalls the restrained gestures of
the figures on Attic grave-stones, and this leads him to mention a theme to
be developed later—the fact that we, unlike the Greeks, cannot find adequate
external symbols for the life within us.

l. 3:   *the days of Tobias*

Rilke is referring to the apocryphal Book of Tobit. Tobit, an Israelite who
had been carried captive to Nineveh, had left a considerable sum of money
with a man in Media, and, feeling the approach of death, ordered his son
Tobias to go and recover it. When Tobias went to seek a man who should
guide him, *he found Raphael that was an angel. But he knew not; and he
said unto him:—'Canst thou go with me to Rages? And knowest thou those*

places well?' The angel replied that he knew the places well and would go with him. *So they went forth both, and the young man's dog with them.*

ll. 37–38: *Lovers, if Angels could understand them, might utter*
                 strange things in the midnight air

We are reminded of the opening lines of the *First Elegy:*
       Who, if I cried, would hear me among the angelic
       orders?

Lovers *might* be able to give some news of us to the Angels, might be able to make the Angels *hear.*

l. 65: *O, how strangely the drinker eludes his part*

The part of the 'pure' lover is to give, to endure as the arrow endures the string, etc., but the requited lover is a taker as well as a giver, a drinker as well as a drink. Campion's lines

       What harvest half so sweet is
       As still to reap the kisses
          Grown ripe in sowing,
       And straight to be receiver
       Of that which thou art giver,
          Rich in bestowing?

would seem to express a different philosophy of love.

ll. 66–67: *On Attic stelês, did not the circumspection*
       of human gesture amaze you

On January 10th, 1912, at the very time when he was writing, or was about to write, these first two *Elegies,* Rilke wrote to Lou Andreas-Salomé, from Duino: *Once in Naples, I believe, in front of some ancient grave-stone, it flashed through me that I ought never to touch people with stronger gestures than were there depicted. And I really believe I sometimes get so far as to express the whole impulse of my heart, without loss and fatality, in gently laying my hand on a shoulder. Would not this, Lou, would not this be the only progress conceivable within that "discretion" you bid me remember?* (*Briefe aus den Jahren 1907–1914,* 160–61.) How significant this image was for Rilke is suggested by two of the *Later Poems,* written, respectively, in 1922 and 1924—*Seek no graver knowledge than the pillar* (174) and *On the sunny road* (85).

l. 75:   *own little strip of orchard*

The German *Fruchtland* reminds us that one of the words Rilke said he envied while writing the *Elegies* was *verger.* (See Introduction, p. 18.)

The Third Elegy

In the *Second Elegy* the inadequacy of ordinary lovers has been suggested; here, the theme is the contrast between that sublime love which is an end in itself, the love of the great feminine lovers such as Gaspara Stampa, celebrated in the *First Elegy,* and the blind animal passion which is always the foundation, and often the whole content, of masculine love.

Here Rilke confronts that physical basis of life which has so often seemed to make Man's higher aspirations meaningless, which held Swift in a condition of fascinated repulsion, and which, at times, seems even to have upset the balance of Shakespeare.

Here, too, another theme is introduced for the first time—the theme of Childhood: not those aspects of it which, in the *Fourth* and *Eighth Elegies,* are revealed for envy and admiration, but its dark miseries and terrors, which even the tenderest maternal love could not dispel. We are reminded of many a passage in *Malte Laurids Brigge,* and of the poem beginning *Don't let the fact that it* WAS,—*Childhood, that nameless bond,* in *Later Poems* (52).

l. 54:   *on whose mute overthrownness*
Rilke used an almost identical phrase and image in a letter to Princess Marie, in 1915: . . . *shall we not even later, for ever, as we are now learning to do, postpone all understanding, regard humanity as inextricable, history as a primeval forest whose floor we never reach, because it stands endlessly, layer upon layer, on what has been overthrown* [auf Gestürztem steht], *an apparition on the back of downfall?* . . . (*Briefe aus den Jahren 1914–1921,* 53.) The original floor or soil of a primeval forest has been buried for ages beneath layers of fallen and decayed trees; what one treads upon in such a forest may therefore be described as 'overthrownness.'

ll. 83–84:   *give him those counter-*
          balancing nights
I am not absolutely certain whether this (a) is the correct translation, or whether the following version (b) would not be more correct:
                    give him preponderance
          over his nights.
I.e., I am not certain whether *Übergewicht* is to be regarded as an attribute of *nights* or of *maiden.* On the whole, one of the *Poems to Night,* written in 1924, seems to support (a). It begins:
          Nacht. O du in Tiefe gelöstes
          Gesicht an meinem Gesicht.

> *Du, meines staunenden Anschauns größtes*
> *Übergewicht.*

which may be literally rendered:

> *Night. O you in depth dissolved*
> *face against my face.*
> *You, my wondering gaze's greatest*
> *counter-weight.*

(In *Later Poems*, 112, a freer translation is given.)

In both poem and *Elegy* Night seems to be thought of as something that outweighs, counter-weighs, preponderates over (1) the poet's gaze, (2) the youth's primeval impulses and terrors. If (a) is correct, a distinction must be made between the dark, terrifying nights endured by the child and the nights which outweigh the day, the countervailing 'lovers' nights' provided by the maiden.

The Fourth Elegy

This, the most bitter and negative of all the *Elegies,* was written in Munich during the autumn of 1915, and something of the mood in which it was composed may be suggested by the concluding phrase of a letter written in August of the same year and quoted in the Commentary on *Later Poems* (230–31)—*the world has fallen into the hands of men.*

Its main theme has already been alluded to in the *First Elegy*—that distractedness, that dividedness of mind, which prevents us from performing our proper task on earth, or, what is the same thing, from surrendering ourselves to those unseen forces whose instruments we are, and only in fulfilling whose purposes we can give a meaning to our lives.

We lack the infallible instinct and the undivided consciousness of the animals (a theme to be developed in the *Eighth Elegy*). Our perpetual awareness of our transitoriness as a limitation prevents us from trying to accept it as a condition. After some fleeting perception of eternity we fall back into the flux of time, and flounder there in a kind of desperate dividedness. No sooner have we concentrated upon one thing than we think of some other thing, to which it is to be a means, or which is to follow it, or which we might have chosen instead. We are perpetually oscillating between what we are doing and what we might be doing, between what we have chosen and what we might have chosen, between what is immediately before us and what is, or may be, just round the corner. We are 'half-filled masks,' only half-heartedly and half-attentively playing the parts allotted to us. A puppet-show is a less depressing spectacle. A puppet's face may be 'all outside,' its inner life may be no more than sawdust, but, at least, it completely fills its part. An Angel could do more with a puppet than, because of our perpetual refractoriness and dividedness, the unseen powers are able to do with us.

But even this most bitter *Elegy* ends with praise, praise of Childhood: could we retain or regain the open and undivided consciousness of the child, distracted neither by past nor by future, surrendering itself entirely to the eternal present, we should be able to play our parts.

l. 1: *O trees of life, when will your winter come*

To say what is the exact 'meaning' of this line is very difficult, for it seems to contain many possible meanings, which must, perhaps, be felt rather than understood. The trees, as autumn moves towards winter, have shed their leaves, the migratory birds are congregating for their flight to warmer climates: when, though, will the 'trees of life' reveal that *their* winter is approaching, and when shall we, like the birds, perceive the signal to depart? A reader unfamiliar with Rilke's thought might suppose that the 'winter' he was longing for was death, liberation from life, eternal repose; we must remember, however, that for him death was not the opposite of life but the other side of life, not a cessation but a transformation. And if we are inclined to believe (as I am) that Princess Marie's statement that Rilke told her that the opening lines of *all* the other *Elegies* were written at Duino during the first weeks of 1912 (*Erinnerungen an Rainer Maria Rilke,* 41) is not to be taken quite literally, that the *whole* of this *Elegy* was written in Munich during the late autumn of 1915, and that, perhaps, as so often happened, the without suddenly responded to the within, and the first line came to him as he was walking in a park among the leafless trees and the congregating birds, we shall, perhaps, more deeply appreciate the longing for change and for the signs of change which it expresses. (See Introduction, p. 11. *During almost all the War-years I was . . . waiting in Munich, always thinking it* MUST *come to an end, not understanding, not understanding, not understanding!*) Nevertheless, it is impossible to nail down the meaning, and some fruitful trains of reflexion may be suggested by the last stanza of the little trilogy *O Lacrimosa . . .* (*Later Poems,* 138), where something of the relationship between Rilke's thoughts about winter and change and death is revealed:

> *Winters, though! That mysterious*
> *hibernation of earth! Where around the dead.*
> *in the sap's pure recession,*
> *boldness accumulates,*
> *boldness of future springs.*

> *Where under rigidity*
> *cogitation goes on. Where green,*
> *worn-out by the big summers,*
> *turns into new*
> *idea and mirror of intimation;*
> *where the colour of flowers*
> *entirely forgets the way our eyes would linger.*

l. 11: *Hostility's our first response*

Hostility, refusal, withdrawal come more naturally to us than self-surrender and co-operation. Cf. the following stanza from the poem *Antistrophes* (*Later Poems*, 92), in which the deficiencies of men are contrasted with the virtues of women:

> *We, vexed by ourselves,*
> *gladly vexing, and gladly*
> *vexed again by our need:*
> *we, like weapons beside*
> *watchfully sleeping rage.*

ll. 21–22:   *The well-known garden,*
     swaying a little

I.e., like a backcloth which has just been put into position.

l. 35:   *the boy with the brown squinting eyes*

His cousin, Egon von Rilke, who died in childhood, and to whose memory the eighth sonnet in the Second Part of the *Sonnets to Orpheus* is dedicated. Rilke wrote of him: *I often think of him and keep on returning to that figure which has remained for me indescribably affecting. Much "childhood," the sadness and helplessness of childhood, is embodied for me in his form, in the ruff he wore, in his little neck, in his chin, in his beautiful brown eyes, disfigured by a squint. So I invoked him once more in connexion with that eighth Sonnet, which expresses transitoriness, after he had already duly served as the prototype for little Erik Brahe, who died as a child, in the "Note-Books of M. L. Brigge."* (Carl Sieber, *René Rilke*, 59–60.)

ll. 65 ff.:   *O hours of childhood,* etc.

In reply to his 'young poet,' who had complained of his loneliness, Rilke wrote, in 1903, that loneliness was not to be regarded as an unfortunate accident, but as a real and necessary task:

What's needed is just this: Loneliness, vast inner loneliness. To walk in oneself and to meet no one for hours on end,—that's what one must be able to attain. To be lonely in the way one was lonely as a child, when the grown-

ups moved about involved in things that appeared important and big be-
cause the big ones looked so busy and because one understood nothing of
what they were doing.

And if, one day, one comes to perceive that their occupations are misera-
ble, their professions moribund and no longer related to life, why not go on
regarding them, like a child, as something alien, looking out from the depth
of one's own world, from the expanse of one's own loneliness, which is it-
self work and rank and profession? Why want to exchange a child's wise
not-understanding for defensiveness and contempt, when not-understanding
means being alone, while defensiveness and contempt mean participation in
that from which one is trying, by their means, to separate oneself? (*Briefe
an einen jungen Dichter*, 31–32.)

l. 73: *within the gap left between world and toy*

For a fuller understanding of Rilke's conception of the part played by toys
in a child's life, the reader may be referred to his essay on Dolls (*Puppen*),
published in 1914 (*Gesammelte Werke*, IV, 265 ff.), and, above all, per-
haps, to the beginning of his second lecture on Rodin, from which some pas-
sages must be quoted. He asks his audience to try to remember something
of their childhood, for he is going to speak to them, not of people, but of
things—*Things, Dinge:* the word, as Rilke uses it, has an almost mystical,
almost magical significance.

*If you can manage it, return with a portion of your weaned and grown-up
feeling to any one of the things of your childhood with which you were much
occupied. Consider whether there was anything at all that was closer, more
intimate, and more necessary to you than such a Thing. Whether everything
—apart from it—was not in a position to hurt or wrong you, to frighten you
with a pain or confuse you with an uncertainty. If kindness was among your
first experiences and confidence and not being alone—are you not indebted
to it? Was it not with a Thing that you first shared your little heart, like a
piece of bread that had to suffice for two? . . .*

*This small forgotten object, that was ready to signify everything, made you
intimate with thousands through playing a thousand parts, being animal
and tree and king and child,—and when it withdrew, they were all there.
This Something, worthless as it was, prepared your relationships with the
world, it guided you into happening and among people, and, further: you
experienced through it, through its existence, through its anyhow-appearance,
through its final smashing or its enigmatic departure, all that is human, right
into the depths of death.* (*Gesammelte Werke*, IV, 377–78.)

ll. 76 ff.: *Who'll show a child just as it is*

This has been generally felt to be one of the most 'difficult' passages in the *Elegies*—largely, perhaps, because readers have tried to translate into concepts what Rilke himself felt to be beyond conception, and, accordingly, contented himself with suggesting by means of images and emblems, so that

sense might judge what phansie could not reach.

In attempting the following brief 'interpretation,' I have owed much to Eberhardt Kretschmar (*Die Weisheit Rainer Maria Rilkes*, 69–71) and Heinrich Cämmerer (*R. M. Rilkes Duineser Elegien: Deutung der Dichtung*, 54–55), but, at the risk, perhaps, of falling into some absurdity, I have tried to avoid abstraction and to make the reader *see*.

Putting questions that are also answers, giving instructions, as it were, to some imaginary painter, with a power, such as Blake's, of making seen what cannot be said, Rilke gropes after an image that shall embody the essence of childhood. Who shall depict a child against the starry background of its own self-sufficient world, with something in its hand—a kind of measuring-rod, perhaps—to indicate the distance between that world and our own? What action or gesture or emblem shall suggest the closeness, the terribly unconscious closeness, of that little life to death? Death, perhaps, shall be represented by a piece of greyish bread which it is holding in its other hand, for, as easily and naturally and unnoticeably as soft bread grows hard, or, even, as bread is eaten, death passes into the life of a child. Or, perhaps, by the core of an apple—a dish of apples standing by suggesting that the child has just eaten one, and its parted lips revealing the presence of a core, which, unlike a grown-up person, it has not ejected (the zeal of grown-ups to banish death from their lives is satirised in the *Tenth Elegy*), and which is going to choke it. (Suggesting, too, that death has always been present in the child, as the core and pips have always been present in the fruit.) The minds and motives, the 'wickedness,' of murderers, who violently bring death upon others, are easily understood, but the 'goodness' of the child, which can allow death to dwell within it even before its life has really begun, is beyond description and comprehension.

The Fifth Elegy

This, the last *Elegy* to be written, was largely inspired by Picasso's picture, *Les Saltimbanques*, reproduced as the frontispiece to this book, and by memories of the real saltimbanques, who, as he told Lou Andreas-Salomé on completing the *Elegy*, had meant so much to him ever since his first days in Paris. (*Briefe aus Muzot,* 104–5.) The *Elegy* is dedicated to the owner of the picture, Frau Hertha Koenig. In June, 1915, while he was living in Munich, and finding it difficult to obtain suitable lodgings, he asked her whether, during the absence of herself and family in the country, he might establish himself for a while in her house in the Widenmayer Strasse, and enjoy the privilege of living beside 'the great Picasso.' His request was granted, and he lived there from June till October. Shortly after moving in, he told a friend that he was living *with the loveliest Picasso* (*the "Saltimbanques"*), *in which there is so much Paris that, for moments, I forget.* (*Briefe aus den Jahren 1914–1921,* 50.)

The reader may be recommended to devote some attention to the reproduction of this picture before reading the poem, although between picture and poem the correspondence is not exact but general. Picasso's six figures are stylised, timeless, and motionless; they are standing in the middle of a landscape, and it is impossible to say whether they are arriving or departing, beginning or ending their performance. Rilke's acrobats are definitely about to begin; they are standing on a 'threadbare carpet,' perhaps in some Parisian suburb, and a number of spectators have gathered round. In the picture appear, from left to right: (1) A powerfully built man in harlequin's dress, who may be identified with 'the youngster, the man' of ll. 34–36, and with the man who, in l. 52, is 'clapping his hands for the downward spring.' (2) A stout man, wearing a conical cap and with a sack over his shoulder, who may have suggested, but certainly cannot be identified with, the 'withered wrinkled lifter,' the former strong man, of l. 27. (3) A slender young man in a bathing-slip, with a drum on his shoulder, who does not appear in the poem, although his drum may have suggested part of the description of the 'lifter,' who is now only good for drumming. (4) A little boy, described in ll. 41–63, looking tenderly, or with what might be tenderness, towards (5) his seldomly tender mother. (6) The little girl, whose hand the leader is holding, referred to in ll. 64–74.

In many ways the acrobats, both in the exercise of their profession and in their relationships with one another, seem to Rilke symbolic of human activity as a whole. Always travelling and with no fixed abode, they are even a shade more fleeting than the rest of us, whose fleetingness was lamented in the *Second Elegy.* Pitifully assembled there on their 'threadbare carpet,' they suggest the ultimate loneliness and isolation of Man in this incomprehensible world. Practising their arduous profession from childhood until death, it is as though they were playthings in the hands of some unknown will; at first, perhaps, they recall the limiting case of Angel and Doll, imagined in the preceding *Elegy,* but the 'emptiness' of their so hardly-conquered skill, which seems to give pleasure neither to them nor to the spectators who come and go like the petals of a rose, suggests rather some Aristophanic jester than the Angel. Significant and characteristic is the fact that Rilke lingers over the sadness of the little boy, jolted back, like the children in the *Fourth* and *Eighth Elegies,* from his approach to reality by the uncomprehending elders, over that sadness which never has time to reach his heart, and that the only thing he selects from this exhibition of empty capability, and offers to the Angel as a token of the divinity in Man, is the smile of tenderness which, in spite of all, is still able to shine through his tears. That life is real in proportion to its difficulty was one of Rilke's most fundamental convictions: accordingly, he tries to imagine the moment when the acrobats still found their performance difficult and, therefore, real; before they had áchieved their present facility, before their 'pure too-little' had passed into this 'empty too-much.' In the *Second Elegy* he had noticed a similar decline in the lives of lovers—how, when they began to receive, they also began to lose the power of giving; he now imagines the acrobats as lovers, or lovers as acrobats. Suppose the true way of conceiving death is not as the 'modiste Madame Lamort,' who makes life seem cheap and meaningless, but as the other side of life, and suppose that there lovers, those ἀθληταὶ τοῦ μεγίστου ἀγῶνος, were able to perform their now insuperable task as easily as these acrobats go through their empty motions: then, indeed, there would be an exhibition of skill that had been worth achieving; then the smile upon the performers' faces would no longer be a false, fixed smile of convention, but a true smile from the heart; and the spectators, the dead, would experience real happiness.

On Rilke's conviction that the true meaning of love could only be understood in relation to death and to 'the Whole,' see Appendix II. See also the poem *Soul in Space (Later Poems,* 94), between which and the latter part of this *Elegy* there is a most striking resemblance.

ll. 14–15:   *the great initial*
               letter of Thereness

Here there is possibly a double meaning which cannot be reproduced in translation. A glance at Picasso's picture will reveal that the five standing figures might be contained within a large capital D, of which the man in harlequin's dress formed the upright and the little boy the extreme end of the loop: D for *Dasein.* (See Eudo C. Mason, *Lebenshaltung und Symbolik bei Rainer Maria Rilke,* Weimar, Verlag Böhlau, 1939, 136.)

ll. 19–26:   *Alas, and round this*
              centre the rose of onlooking, etc.

The 'centre' of interest is the group of four (not, as in the picture, five)
acrobats (excluding the woman): they are referred to, collectively, as the
'pestle,' because they are always pounding their threadbare carpet, and as
the 'pistil,' because around them the onlookers come and go like the petals
of a rose around the pistil, or cluster of carpels. The way in which the meta-
phor is worked out may be shown by means of the following parallel col-
umns:

Petals	Onlookers
Pistil	Pestle (the four acrobats)
Pollen	Dust (raised by the 'pestle.' *Staub* can mean both 'dust' and 'pol-len.')
Sham-fruit	Boredom (sham-pleasure)
Shining surface of fruit	Superficial smile of performers and onlookers.

ll. 34–35:   *And the youngster, the man, like the son of a neck*
              and a nun

The description would suit the man in harlequin's dress, but certainly not
the young man with the drum on his shoulder. J. F. Angelloz has suggested
that it is as though Rilke's beloved Portuguese Nun (see Appendix I) had
had a son by the oafish Comte de Chamilly. Just as Meredith's Sir Willoughby
Patterne was said to 'have a leg,' so Baron Ochs von Lerchenau and his like
might be said to 'have a neck,' or even to *be* a neck.

ll. 41 ff.: *You, that fall with the thud*
The little boy.

ll. 43–44:   *the tree*
             of mutually built up motion
The human tree, or pyramid, formed by the acrobats.

l. 63:   *"Subrisio Saltat."*

First, the association of images must be observed: 'herb of healing,' herb-
alist, apothecary: the Angel is to place the smile in a vase or urn (possibly
suggested by the jar standing beside the woman) and set it upon a shelf,
with an inscription in abbreviated Latin, like those on the bottles and jars
in a chemist's shop. Written in full, the inscription would read: *Subrisio*
Saltatoris, Acrobat's Smile. The late Latin form *subrisio* (first used by St.

Jerome, in the fourth century) is closer than *risus* to the Italian *sorriso*, a word of which Rilke was very fond.

ll. 64 ff.:   *Then you, my darling*
The little girl.

The Sixth Elegy

In the *First Elegy* Rilke had insisted on the destinies of the great lovers and of the early-departed as keys to the understanding of life and death as aspects of one great unity. In that *Elegy* he had suggested that the existence of the early-departed in our minds and in our hearts was more intense and real than when they were on earth, and at the end of the preceding *Elegy* the aspirations of lovers, which can never be realised on earth, have been celebrated as the preparation for a fuller and intenser life in 'the Whole.' In the present *Elegy* he celebrates the single-hearted and single-minded Hero, whose destiny is strangely akin to that of the early-departed.

The flowering of life in time is but a preparation for its fruit, which is death, conceived, not as the opposite of life, but as its other, its unilluminated side. Most of us, however, draw a sharp distinction between life and death; for us, the great thing is to 'live,' that is, to 'flower,' as long as possible: death, which we fear, and regard as the opposite of life, appears to us as *that ugly cup with the broken handle and the meaningless inscription "Faith Love Hope," from which a bitterness of undiluted death is to be drunk.* (See the poem *Death,* in *Later Poems,* 72, and the Commentary thereon.) The Hero, on the contrary, is indifferent to mere duration; he cares only for existence, which is independent of time. Into the ripe fruit of his death he carries, like the fig tree, a pure and undivulged secret; all our secrets, however, have been already betrayed, we have no further, hidden, significance or intensity, that requires 'the Whole' for its realisation, when at last we enter 'the retarded core of our ultimate fruit.'

In *Later Poems,* 144, there is a sonnet on the Hero.

l. 13:   *that already they're stationed and glowing in fulness of heart*
Cf. R. L. Nettleship: *Fear of death, or clinging to life, is fear of, or clinging to, certain fragments of ourselves. If we could 'energize' a great deal more continuously than most of us can, we might experience physical death literally without being aware of it.* (*Philosophical Remains of Richard Lewis Nettleship,* 2nd ed., 1901, 93.)

l. 31:   *propped upon arms still to be*
Arms which, to speak philosophically, and, perhaps, a trifle pedantically,

have not yet realised their potentiality—little arms that, one day, will be big and strong like Samson's. The boy is buried in his book, his chin in his hands, his elbows resting on his knees or on the table.

The Seventh Elegy

The transition from the *Sixth* to the *Seventh Elegy* has been admirably indicated by Dr. E. L. Stahl. For the Hero life is only a beginning. *But lest this should be thought to mean that life must be rejected as an unnecessary and disconcerting impediment on the path to death, the* SEVENTH ELEGY *immediately proceeds to the glorification of existence. At the point when the value of human life in this world seems to have been completely denied, Rilke proclaims its virtues. Arriving at the furthest possibility of negation, he affirms: "Hiersein ist herrlich." The tide of his poetry is on the turn from lament to praise. (The Duineser Elegien, in Rainer Maria Rilke: Aspects of His Mind and Poetry, Sidgwick and Jackson, 1938, 149.)*

In the *First Elegy* Rilke had suggested that Man's real function or mission might, perhaps, be closely connected with the fact of his transitoriness, might be nothing other than to give the highest possible significance to his moments as they passed, but that from the constant alertness and receptivity which this task required he (i.e., as so often, Rilke *qua* Man, or Man *qua* Rilke) was perpetually distracted by a longing for some permanently satisfying possession, for some ideal companion. He now declares that he has outgrown this longing:

> *Not wooing, no longer shall wooing, voice that's outgrown it,*
> *be now the form of your cry.*

We are reminded of one of the *Sonnets to Orpheus* (I, 3), where it is declared that real song is not *Werbung um ein endlich noch Erreichtes,* 'wooing of something finally attained,' but *Dasein,* 'existence.' Not that he no longer has the power to woo, but that, if he did so now, his wooing would be as pure and impersonal as that of a bird caught up by the surging Spring. If desire were present, it would be a kind of universal desire, not limited to a particular object, for it would be at the same time an annunciation of the blessedness of existence. More than that longed-for, unknown beloved, the possibility of whose existence, as Rilke had declared in one of the *Later Poems* (*Shatter me, music,* 99), would depend on his being able to

> *extort resounding storms*
> *from the trumpet an angel blows on high at the end of the world*

would respond to it: those early-departed, who, as he had declared in the

First Elegy, seemed always to be waiting for him to remove that appearance of suffered injustice which hindered their progress in eternity, would gather to hear the voice of one who had come to understand life through death and death through life; who had come to perceive that the value of life depended, not on its duration, but on its intensity. 'Apparently' the youthfully-dead were cut off before they had had their fill of happiness, and often the happiness they enjoyed was not 'apparent'; but the truest happiness is never apparent, for it is something invisible, something within.

At this point, what had been lamented at the end of the *Second Elegy* is now regarded as a matter for rejoicing: although we, unlike the Greeks and the people of former ages, can no longer find external equivalents for our innermost feelings and aspirations, we are in a position to perceive more clearly that our real task is one of transformation—transformation of the visible world outside us into an invisible world within. And the fact that such experienceable things as our forefathers knew are becoming fewer and fewer impels us to preserve, by transforming them into an imperishable invisibility, the significance of those great visible achievements that still remain.

l. 36: *Don't think Destiny's more than what's packed into childhood*
Nearly twenty years earlier Rilke had written to the 'young poet':

It's necessary—and this is the direction which, little by little, our evolution will take—that nothing alien should befall us, but only what has long been ours. So many concepts of motion have had to be re-thought, that it will also come to be recognised, gradually, that what we call destiny comes out of people, not into them from outside. Only because so many people, all the time their destinies were living inside them, did not absorb them and transform them into themselves, have they failed to recognise what came out of them; it was so strange to them, they supposed, in their confused terror, that it had got into them at that very moment, for they swore they had never found anything like that in themselves before. Just as for a long time people deceived themselves about the motion of the sun, they are still deceiving themselves about the motion of what's to come. The future is stationary, dear Herr Kappus, but we are moving in infinite space. (Briefe an einen jungen Dichter, 45.)

Cf. also the poem in *Later Poems* (52), which was originally intended for a place among the *Elegies,* and which begins:

Don't let the fact that it was,*—Childhood, that nameless bond between Heaven and us,—ever be cancelled by fate.*

The Eighth Elegy

The current of praise that was rising so powerfully in the preceding *Elegy* is again interrupted by lament. Already certain fundamental defects or weaknesses in human nature have been lamented: our transitoriness, our inability to accept it as a condition, our distractedness and half-heartedness, our fear of death; but, at the same time, there has been some suggestion that these weaknesses are not insuperable—Rilke now insists upon a still more fundamental defect or limitation—the fact that in almost all consciousness there is a distinction between what philosophers call subject and object: the fact that our awareness of Being, or existence, as an object, as something distinct from ourselves, prevents us from identifying ourselves with it and achieving a condition of pure Being or pure existence. Being or existence perceived as something not-ourselves, Rilke calls 'World,' and contrasts with what he calls 'the open,' the 'nowhere without no.' In this 'open' world there is no time, no past or future, no end, no limit, no separation or parting, and no death as the opposite of life. Children sometimes enter this condition of timeless Being, but are always jogged back again; lovers draw near to it, but are distracted by the interposing presence of their partners in love; even the animals, who seem always to be looking and moving *towards* that openness from which we are always looking and moving *away,* are sad with the memory of a more intimate life in the womb. Those moments in which the distinction between subject and object is transcended and the barriers of selfhood completely broken down—moments such as those described by Rilke in the fragment *Experience* and elsewhere (see Appendix III)—are few and fleeting and far between: they reveal to us our true home, from which, however, like departing travellers, we are for ever taking leave.

The *Elegy* is dedicated to Rilke's friend Rudolf Kassner, an Austrian writer whose difficult but fascinating books are almost unknown in England. In 1926 and 1935 Kassner published two very interesting and important essays on Rilke, which have lately been republished together in his *Buch der Erinnerung* (Insel-Verlag, 1938). In these essays personal recollection and generous appreciation are mingled with sharp and often shrewd criticism of Rilke's attitude to life. The most fundamental concept among Kassner's characteristic convictions and ideas is that of *Umkehr,* or Conversion, by means of which he tries to indicate the true line of development in Western civilisation and to defend it against what seem to him atavistic revivals or attacks. The exemplary modern man has been 'converted' from the almost purely external, finite, static, 'space-world' of God the Father, of number or quantity, of identity, of discontinuity, of magic, of chance, of happiness, to the more internal, more spiritual, infinite, dynamic, 'time-world' of the Son, of quality, of individuality, of continuity and rhythm, of order and system, of freedom, of sacrifice. *Conversion,* he writes, in *Zahl und Gesicht* (an untranslatable phrase, which may be roughly rendered *Quantity and Quality*), *means, lastly and most profoundly, that we do not construct the world on any identity, whether we call this identity Will, God, Thing in itself, Duration, Primal cell, or anything else. Conversion is thus the centre of an infinite world, of a world in motion. Whoever in his soul revolts against or shocks an identity, whoever in his soul revolts against chance or a coming into existence through chance, is a convert, or feels the necessity of conversion. He is truly in motion.* (231.)

Rilke, so it seemed to Kassner, was unconverted: he belonged to the 'space-world,' the world of God the Father. In his first essay (1926) he wrote:

He did not want sacrifice, or, rather, he wanted the sacrifice of the Old Testament (the fruits of the field, a lamb, or whatever else is dear to men), but not that of the New. He did not want us to be able to win measure only from sacrifice, through conversion. Read the eighth of the Duino Elegies. *It is dedicated to me and is directed against the conception of conversion which he met with in my books. The animal does not turn round, the animal lives in the world of the Father. The greatness of the Father-world was still entirely contained in Being; that is quite true. With the Son greatness is detached from Being. The Son is great, but the Father* is. *Rilke was not without rancour against the Son. Examples thereof are certain poems in the second volume of* New Poems. (296.)

In his second essay (1935) Kassner again refers to the *Eighth Elegy:*

I well remember how he spoke to me about this inner happiness of the gnat, many years before the composition of the Elegy, in one of those conversations in the preserve at Duino, during which there was also talk of the Mediator and of mediation and of his attitude thereto. The dedication is probably connected with this, as well as with certain passages in my Outlines of a Universal Physiognomy, the introduction to Zahl und Gesicht. (317.)

It would be impossible to go further into this subject without a detailed exposition of some of Kassner's leading ideas; it must suffice to say that the limitations and contradictions which Rilke laments in this *Elegy* seemed to Kassner necessary conditions of life in the time-world, the world of the Son, of individuality, of freedom, suffering, and sacrifice, and that Rilke's longing for 'the open' seemed to him a kind of atavism.

l. 1:   *the creature-world*

At the conclusion of an important letter on spiritualism, written in 1924, Rilke recommends to his correspondent, among those 'normal' counterpoises which should enable us to accept as a matter of course the apparently 'abnormal' apparitions, the animals: *These, indeed, these confidants of the Whole, the animals, who are most at home in a broader segment of consciousness, most readily conduct us, once again—across, and are near to the medial condition.* (*Briefe aus Muzot*, 283–84.)

ll. 38–40:   *But its own being for it*
      is infinite, inapprehensible,
      unintrospective, pure, like its outward gaze

Dr. Eberhardt Kretschmar's observations on these lines are well worth quoting:

Perhaps it is not entirely superfluous to remark that these reflexions and words of Rilke's are not the mere speculations and fancies of a poet remote from the world, but possess full reality and are the result of a quite uncommon and quite sober observation of nature. If, without any preconception, we look any animal in the eyes, a dog or a horse or a bird, we shall see that their look, their outlook, simply does not meet our eyes and our look, and that even the "true dog-eyes" keep only just on the surface of this animal's real look and being, and that every animal's look, even when it is looking at us, looks out beyond us, away beyond us, and through and through us into immeasurable distances, into the open, into pure space, and that this look is the expression of the entire animal existence,—an existence that is precisely as Rilke has described it: infinite, inapprehensible. (Die Weisheit Rainer Maria Rilkes, 126.)

ll. 43–44: *And yet, within the wakefully-warm beast*
      there lies the weight and care of a great sadness

Its perpetual wakefulness is regarded as a consequence of its warmbloodedness. In 1924, Rilke wrote that in the baths of Ragaz, whose temperature was almost exactly that of the human body, one enjoyed *something of the extended feeling of those creatures whose bodily temperature adjusts itself to whatever medium surrounds them.* (*Briefe aus Muzot*, 286.)

With regard to the next line, Dr. Kretschmar is again worth quoting:

Even these words are no irresponsible speculations; they, too, are confirmed by reality. For if we only observe any animal, a deer, for example, or a horse—not an old worn-out creature, but a blood-horse, say, in one of the East Prussian studs—or if we even look at pictures of beasts of prey in the jungle, it will very soon become clear to us that—in an entirely unsenti-mental sense—there is nothing sadder than the face of an animal, any ani-mal. This so clearly perceptible metaphysical sadness is what Rilke means in the verses quoted. (Op. cit., 128.)

ll. 52–53:   *O bliss of* TINY *creatures that* REMAIN
              for ever in the womb that brought them forth

In 1918 he wrote to Lou Andreas-Salomé: . . . *That a multitude of crea-tures, which proceed from externally exposed seed, should have* THAT *for ma-ternal body, this spacious, excitable open,—how at home they must feel in it their whole lives longl Why, they do nothing but leap for joy in their moth-er's womb, like little John the Baptist; for this same space has both conceived them and brought them forth, they never come out of its security at all. (Briefe aus den Jahren 1914–1921, 177–78.)*

ll. 58–60:   *like one of those Etruscan souls,* etc.

On the walls of their sarcophagus chambers the Etruscans depicted the soul as a bird, and on the sarcophagus itself there often reposed a life-size figure of the dead. The soul, therefore, has escaped from the body, but is also excluded from it, just as the bird may be said to have escaped, and also to be excluded from, the egg. It is this feeling of exclusion that robs it of full assurance.

The Ninth Elegy

In the preceding *Elegy* the contradictions in human nature and the sad-ness of human destiny have been lamented, and the lament is continued in the question with which the present *Elegy* begins. This beginning, it should be remembered, was possibly written at Duino: we may imagine the poet resting his gaze upon the cool, green laurels in the castle park, recalling, perhaps, the transformation of Daphne, and speculating for a moment on the superior felicity of arboreal existence to human destiny, which, in the preceding *Elegy,* has been described as

> *being opposite,*
> *and nothing else, and always opposite.*

(Attempts to discover some more esoteric symbolism in the 'laurel' are prob-ably mistaken. Rivers, the psychologist, records the case-history of a man who believed he was a duck: in a moment of depression and anxiety he had found relief in contemplating these creatures, and had ended by identifying himself with them. After all, we have heard Rilke envying the happiness of the gnatl) Why, in spite of all, he asks, when the choice is offered to me, do

I still choose to persist with this human destiny? (No pronoun, it is true, appears until the tenth line, and then it is the first person plural, but, in spite of this show of impersonality, this is, perhaps, the most personal of all the *Elegies*, the one in which the 'We' is most obviously an 'I.') The reply had already been suggested in the *First Elegy*, in the words

All this was a trust;

it had almost been formulated at the end of the *Seventh*; and, in prose, it is given as fully and clearly as possible in the letter to his Polish translator, quoted in Appendix IV. We are finite, we are transitory, we are perpetually conscious of an opposite, of something not ourselves: looked at in one way, these are limitations and matter for regret; looked at in another way, they are conditions and matter for rejoicing—conditions, that is to say, for the fulfilment of our specifically human task, that of transformation. Only in and through the finite consciousnesses of a succession of transitory beings like ourselves could the visible world be re-created into an invisible one, could 'externality,' in the words of a modern philosopher, be 'raised towards the Absolute.' Transitoriness, therefore, is no longer regretted as a limitation, but joyfully accepted as a condition: negation is overcome by affirmation, and affirmation is strengthened by what it has overcome. And in this complete dedication and submission to the specifically human, the specifically finite, task, freedom is found, freedom from fear—above all, from fear of death; for death, through whom the process of transformation, both here and beyond, is continued, is regarded no longer as an enemy, but as a friend. And, finally, by a kind of coincidence of opposites, the finite achieves infinity and the transient, eternity; for what is the present, the here and now, completely accepted, completely affirmed, but the eternal present, but eternity, infinity, itself?

Thus, to the agonised question of the *First Elegy*:

Alas, who is there

we can make use of?

the reply is given: No one; but there are powers by which, if we submit ourselves to them, we can be used. This, too, is the conclusion of one of the most memorable *Sonnets to Orpheus* (II, 27):

Ach, das Gespenst des Vergänglichen,
durch den arglos Empfänglichen
geht es, als wär es ein Rauch.

Als die, die wir sind, als die Treibenden,
gelten wir doch bei bleibenden
Kräften als göttlicher Brauch.

which may be roughly rendered:

> *Spectre of mortal fragility,*
> *simply-receptive docility*
> *smiles when your shadow descends.*

> *We can be, with our waxing and waning,*
> *fitlier used by remaining*
> *forces for ultimate ends.*

Indeed, it is in this *Ninth Elegy* that the *Duino Elegies,* whose predominant theme is Lament (*Klage*), approach most nearly to the *Sonnets to Orpheus,* whose predominant theme is Praise (*Rühmung*). The *Sonnets to Orpheus,* which were begun shortly before the completion of the *Elegies,* in February, 1922, and finished shortly afterwards, came to Rilke as a surprise; but that they represented no sudden change or development, and that they had been as potentially present in him during all these years as the predominantly mournful *Elegies,* is revealed by a letter he wrote, in October, 1918, to his friend, Countess Aline Dietrichstein. Although, he declared, she had only known him during the War years, and had constantly heard him deploring the 'indescribable numbness and inhibition,' the joylessness, which he suffered more than most, he had, nevertheless, never lost his faith in the essential goodness of life. *During all these years I have not asked myself (it would have been imprudent to do so) how deeply, in spite of all the misery, confusion, and disfigurement in the world, I still believe in the vast, entire, far-inexhaustible possibilities of life. Your wedding-day shall be the occasion for me to examine myself. And I now confess, dear Countess, that I regard life as a thing of the most unimpeachable deliciousness, and that the intrication of so many fatalities and horrors, the sacrifice of such numerous destinies, all that has insuperably grown up for us during these last years into an ever-increasing terror, cannot confuse my judgment about the fullness and goodness and affectionateness of existence. (Briefe aus den Jahren 1914–1921, 203.)*

l. 79:   *Supernumerous existence*
The word *überzählig* is here used by Rilke, not in its ordinary sense, but with the meaning: beyond the realm or reach of number; timeless, infinite.

The Tenth Elegy

In the preceding *Elegy* the transitoriness of human life has been accepted and celebrated as the condition of Man's specific function and activity in relation to 'the Whole.' In this, the last *Elegy*, the most difficult of all affirmations is attempted—that of sorrow and suffering in general. The opening lines, celebrating the ultimate triumph of suffering, or of insight into the nature of suffering, are among the most exultantly and compellingly jubilant Rilke ever wrote. They had been composed ten years before, at Duino, and how ardently he hoped to achieve the insight there momentarily captured is revealed in a letter he wrote some months later to warn a young admirer that what she called his 'world' was still incomplete: *Just now I am more than ever in one-sidedness: lamentation has frequently preponderated; yet I know that one is justified in making such full use of the strings of lamentation only if one has resolved to play on them, later too, by means of them, the whole of that triumphant jubilation that swells up behind everything hard and painful and endured, and without which voices are incomplete. (Briefe aus den Jahren 1907–1914, 254.)*

As may be seen from many passages in Rilke's letters, one of his main purposes in the *Elegies* was 'to keep life open towards death' (*Briefe aus Muzot*, 220) and to show the true meaning of love and other human activities, as well as of pain and sorrow, within this extended whole, 'this now first *whole*, first *hale* world' (*op. cit.*, 333). In the *First Elegy*, where almost all the succeeding themes were either stated or implied, it had been suggested that reflexion on the destinies of those who had died young might give us an intuition into the unity of life and death and into the complementariness of sorrow and joy. This theme, which has often reappeared, is now fully developed.

Rilke collects and satirises, in the image or parable of the City of Pain, all that most repelled him in that half-hearted and half-minded kind of life which had for so long been the object of his satire and astonishment—that half-life from which death, and all that is mysterious and inexplicable, is simply excluded; that life whose consolations are provided by conventional religion, and whose activities are the pursuit of happiness and the making of money; from which fear and mystery are banished by distractions, and where suffering is regarded merely as an unfortunate accident. With this half-life, with this enclosed and limited City of Pain, he contrasts the spacious Land of Pain, which is Death, or, rather, that great unity which includes both Life and Death, where the real meaning (the 'flowering') of sadness is perceived, where, instead of a perpetual escape from reality through distractions, there is a perpetual progress in reality through painfully achieved insight, and where, at last, the 'source of joy' is discovered.

The imagery in the latter part of this *Elegy* is drawn largely from Rilke's recollections of Egypt, which he visited during the winter of 1910–11, and of his studies in Egyptology. After describing to his Polish translator his conception of the relationship between life and death and between the visible and the invisible, he declared that the *Elegies cautiously relate it to its origins, claiming primeval traditions and rumours of traditions as support for this conjecture, invoking even in the Egyptian cult of the dead a foreknowledge of such relationships. (Although the "Lament-land," through which the elder "Lament" guides the dead youth, is* NOT *to be* IDENTIFIED *with Egypt, but only to be regarded as a kind of reflexion of the Nile country into the desert-clarity of the dead's consciousness.) (Briefe aus Muzot,* 336–37.)

ll. 48–49: *Only the youthfully-dead, in their first condition*
            of timeless serenity, that of being weaned
Weaned, that is to say, from terrestrial things. Cf. *First Elegy,* ll. 75 ff.:
            Strange, not to go on wishing one's wishes, etc.

l. 70: *scrawls the far-stretching screed of its lonely cry*
See the second half of the next note.

ll. 82–87: *frightens an owl from behind the pschent. And the bird,* etc.
The *pschent* is the double-crown of Upper and Lower Egypt, worn (fragmentarily now) by the Sphinx and by all those rulers who, after the union of the two lands, styled themselves Kings of the South and of the North.

The best commentary on the rest of this passage, as well as on l. 70, is the essay entitled *Ur-Geräusch, Elemental Sound,* which Rilke published in 1919. It begins with a schoolboy recollection—how a master, with a scientific bent, encouraged his pupils to construct a primitive phonograph; how, more than the actual sound produced, the grooves cut on the wax cylinder remained in the memory of the young Rilke (or of his imaginary narrator); and how, years later, when he came to study anatomy, the phenomenon that most impressed him was the coronal suture, which, by a curious association of ideas, recalled the grooves in that primitive gramophone record. Why not make the gramophone needle traverse, not merely grooves produced by sound-vibrations, but some natural object—the coronal suture, for example?—

What would happen?—There would necessarily be a sound, a succession of sounds, a music . . .

Feelings—what? Incredulity, timidity, fear, awe:—yes, which of all immediately possible feelings prevents me from proposing a name for the elemental sound which would thus enter the world? . . .

Putting this aside for a moment: what lines, occurring no matter where, might not be placed thereunder and submitted to the test? What contour

*might not in this way be, as it were, prolonged, so that we might then, after
its transformation, feel it impinging upon us within the realm of another
sense?* (*Gesammelte Werke*, IV, 290.) The immediate purpose of this essay,
to which Rilke attached considerable importance, is to insist that the poet
should try, so far as possible, to apprehend every object through each of the
five senses, and not content himself, as most poets do, with the sense of sight;
and the fundamental idea or intuition behind it is that of a permanent and
unchanging 'content' which may be apprehended under many different
'forms.' That this idea is not, as Rilke himself declared, so fantastic after all
(*Briefe aus Muzot*, 384) is suggested by the fact that people with no theories
on the subject habitually speak of a 'screaming' red or a 'shrill' green, of
orchestral 'colour,' which may be 'dark' or 'bright,' of a melody which is
'sweet' or 'sickly,' or of a sight which is 'touching.'

Here, in order to suggest the extended consciousness of the dead, he makes
the youth able to *see* the cry of a bird and to *hear*, by means of the soundless
flight of the owl which has brushed across its cheek, the outline of the
Sphinx's face.

ll. 88–92:   *And, higher, the stars. New ones. Stars of the Land of Pain*, etc.
The 'Rider' is hardly intelligible without a knowledge of one of the *Son-
nets to Orpheus* (I, 11), where human nature is symbolised by a horse, and
the unseen power that uses and directs it by a rider:

> *Look at the sky. Is there no "Horse-man" reckoned
> among the constellations? For we share
> much with that earth-proud first. And with the second,
> that curbing rider, whom it has to bear.*

> *Is not just this,—first hunted and then broken,
> the sinewy nature of the course we run?
> Turf and turning. Pressure, nothing spoken.
> New horizons. And the two are one.*

> *Are they, though? Or are they never able
> to feel at one about their mutual way?
> So severed from the first by field and table.*

> *Their stellar unity's deceptive too.
> Well, let us find such pleasure as we may
> believing in the figure. That will do.*

The best interpretation of the other symbolic stars is that of H. Cämmerer, to whom, in the following brief observations, I am much indebted.

The 'Staff,' both as cudgel and as pilgrim's staff, and the ripe 'Fruit-garland' are symbols for the hardness and heaviness of life. The 'Cradle' is a symbol for birth and death. The 'Way,' often sought for and found rarely or not at all, is the Way of Life. The terrible 'Burning Book' is a symbol of revelation. It was the 'Doll' which, by playing so many parts, prepared the child for real life. (See Commentary on l. 73 of the *Fourth Elegy*.) The 'Window' is a symbol for longing and expectation, disappointment and parting: cf. the little cycle of French poems entitled *Les Fenêtres* (*Poèmes Français*, Paris, Paul Hartmann, 1935, 97 ff.), of which the fourth begins:

> *Fenêtre, toi, ô mesure d'attente,*
> *tant de fois remplie,*
> *quand une vie se verse et s'impatiente*
> *vers une autre vie.*

Cf. also *Second Elegy*, l. 61, *the window-longing*.

ll. 110–11: *And we, who have always thought*
              of happiness climbing

Referring back to the 'he climbs' of l. 104 and the 'yet' of l. 106. The happiness of the dead is passive rather than what we commonly understand by active; it consists in complete submission to universal law, in their allowing themselves to fall into the depths of Being, into that 'open' from which, as was lamented in the *Fourth Elegy*, we are always turning away. In the poem *Orpheus. Eurydice. Hermes.* it is said of the unwillingly returning Eurydice that

> *she was already loosened like long hair,*
> *and given far and wide like fallen rain*

and in the *Stunden-Buch* (*Gesammelte Werke*, II, 246) it is said of man:

> *Eins muß er wieder können: fallen,*
> *geduldig in der Schwere ruhn,*
> *der sich vermaß, den Vögeln allen*
> *im Fliegen es zuvorzutun.*

There is one thing he must again grow capable of:
falling, patiently resting in heaviness,—he who presumed
to surpass all the birds in flying.

Appendix 1

The Great Lovers

THE following letter, written from Schloss Duino in January, 1912, only two days after he had sent the *First Elegy* to Princess Marie, reveals what Rilke understood by 'the great lovers,' and contains, perhaps, the completest expression of his conception of love.

And then: I have no window on human beings, definitely. They yield themselves to me only in so far as they are able to make themselves heard within myself, and, during these last years, they have been communicating with me almost entirely through two figures, on which I base my conjectures about human beings in general. What speaks to me of humanity, immensely, with a calmness of authority that makes my hearing spacious, is the phenomenon of those who have died young, and, still more unconditionally, purely, inexhaustibly: THE WOMAN WHO LOVES. *In these two forms humanity gets mixed into my heart whether I will or no. They make their appearance in me both with the clearness of the marionette (which is an exterior charged with conviction), and as finished types, which can no longer be improved upon, so that the natural history of their souls might be written.*

Let us keep to the woman who loves,—by whom I don't so much mean St. Theresa and such magnificence as has occurred in that direction: she yields herself to my observation much more unambiguously, purely, i.e. undilutedly, and (so to speak) UNAPPLIEDLY *in the situation of Gaspara Stampa, the Lyonnaise Labé, certain Venetian courtesans, and, above all, Marianna Alcoforado, that incomparable creature, in whose eight heavy letters woman's love is for the first time plotted from point to point, without display, without exaggeration or mitigation, as by the hand of a sibyl. And there, my God, there the fact is revealed that, as the result of the irrepressible logic of the feminine heart, this line was finished, completed, not to be carried any further in the terrestrial sphere, and could only be prolonged into infinity, towards the divine. Nay, there, in the example of this highly irrelevant Chamilly (whose foolish vanity was used by Nature to preserve the Portuguese's letters), with the sublime expression of the nun: "My love no longer depends on the way you treat me"—Man, as a lover, was done with, finished with, OUTLOVED—if one may put it so considerately—outloved, as a glove is outworn . . . What a melancholy figure he cuts in the history of love: he has almost no strength there beyond the superiority which tradition ascribes to him, and even this he carries with a negligence that would be simply revolting, were it not that his absent-mindedness and absent-heartedness have often had great occasions, which partly justify him. No one, however, will persuade me out of what becomes apparent in the case of this extremest lover and her ignominious partner: the fact that this relationship definitely brings to light how very much on one side, that of woman, everything performed, endured, accomplished contrasts with man's absolute insufficiency in love. She receives, as it were—to put the matter with banal clarity—the Diploma of Proficiency in Love, while he carries in his pocket an Elementary Grammar of this discipline, from which a few words have scantily passed into him, out of which, as opportunity offers, he forms sentences, beautiful and ravishing as the well-known sentences on the first pages of Language Courses for Beginners.—The case of the Portuguese is so wonderfully pure because she does not fling the streams of her feeling on in to the imaginary, but, with infinite power, conducts the geniality of this feeling back into herself: enduring it, nothing but that. She grows old in the convent, very old, she becomes no saint, not even a good nun. It is repugnant to her singular tact to apply to God what was not intended for him from the beginning, and what the Comte de Chamilly could disdain. And yet it was almost impossible to check the heroic onrush of this love before the final leap, and not, in the course of such a vibration of one's innermost being, to become a saint. Had she—creature glorious beyond measure!—yielded for one moment, she would have plunged into God like a stone into the sea; and had it pleased God to* attempt with her what he continually does with the angels, casting their whole effulgence back into themselves,—I am certain that, forthwith, just as she was, in this sad convent, she would have become an angel, within, in the depths of her nature. (*Briefe aus den Jahren 1907–1914*, 175–78.)

Appendix 2

Love and Death

RILKE frequently declared that his purpose in the *Elegies* was, not only to represent death as the other, the unilluminated, side of life, but also to show the true place of love within this extended whole, 'this now first *whole*, first *hale* world.' How closely his thoughts about death and his thoughts about love were related may be seen from a letter he wrote, in 1920, to a young wife who had been forsaken. In reply to her bitter question, whether all the labour of loving and all the pain of unrequited love was merely for the purpose of giving life to a child, he admitted that it was indeed a terrifying thought, that the moment of love, which we regard as something so personal, so much our own, might yet be so entirely determined by past and future, and so regardless of the individual. But, he added, even if this were true, there would still remain in the experience an indescribable *depth,* through which we might escape from such terrifying impersonality. *This would agree with the experience, how much every one of our deepest raptures makes itself independent of duration and passage; indeed, they stand vertically upon the courses of life, just as death, too, stands vertically upon them; they have more in common with death than with all the aims and movements of our vitality. Only from the side of death (when death is not accepted as an extinction, but imagined as an altogether surpassing intensity), only from the side of death, I believe, is it possible to do justice to love.* (*Briefe an eine junge Frau,* 21–22.) A further hint as to his meaning is contained in a letter of consolation to the fiancée of his young friend, Norbert von Hellingrath, who had been killed in action at Verdun: *It lies in the nature of every ultimate love that, sooner or later, it is only able to reach the loved one in the infinite. May your deep intellectual community with Norbert and your youth finally help you to see in your fate no revocation, but only this extremest, greatest,—this inexhaustible task. (Briefe aus den Jahren 1914–1921, 125.)* Love, like death, he regarded as an extension of human life into the infinite, as a snatching-up of it into the great cycle, as a plunging of it into the eternal stream. Its passion and hunger cannot and should not (so he always felt) be satisfied by the object that awakens it; it is for something infinite, it extends beyond this visible 'side of life' into the reverted, invisible side we call death, it can find its fulfilment only in 'the Whole.'

Appendix 3

Rilke's Mystical Experiences

RILKE, like D. H. Lawrence, had an extraordinary sensitiveness to what Wordsworth called 'unknown modes of being,' and to what Aldous Huxley, describing Lawrence's special and characteristic gift, calls 'otherness.' He attached great importance to certain mystical or semi-mystical experiences, the most remarkable of which happened to him in the garden of Schloss Duino, in 1912. A year later, in Spain, he tried to describe it as accurately as possible, under the title *Erlebnis* (*Experience*), whereby, as he said, "the domains of the sayable did not really seem to suffice." (*Briefe aus den Jahren 1914–1921*, 227.) Nothing reveals more clearly the kind of 'otherness' with which he became more and more preoccupied during his later years.

It could have been little more than a year ago, when, in the castle garden which sloped down fairly steeply towards the sea, something strange encountered him. Walking up and down with a book, as was his custom, he had happened to recline into the more or less shoulder-high fork of a shrublike tree, and in this position immediately felt himself so agreeably supported and so amply reposed, that he remained as he was, without reading, completely received into nature, in an almost unconscious contemplation. Little by little his attention awoke to a feeling he had never known: it was as though almost imperceptible vibrations were passing into him from the interior of the tree . . . It seemed to him that he had never been filled with more gentle motions, his body was being somehow treated like a soul, and put in a state to receive a degree of influence which, given the normal apparentness of one's physical conditions, really could not have been felt at all . . . Nevertheless, concerned as he always was to account to himself for precisely the most delicate impressions, he insistently asked himself what was happening to him then, and almost at once found an expression that satisfied him, saying to himself, that he had got to the other side of Nature. As sometimes happens in a dream, this phrase now gave him pleasure, and he regarded it as almost unreservedly right. Everywhere and more and more regularly filled with this impulse that kept on recurring in strangely interior intervals, his body became indescribably touching to him and of no further use than to be purely and cautiously present in, just as a ghost, already dwelling elsewhere, sadly enters what has been tenderly laid aside, in order to belong once more, even though inattentively, to this once so indispensable world. Looking slowly around him, without otherwise changing his position, he recognised it all, recalled it, smiled at it with a kind of distant affection, let it be, like something much earlier that once, in circumstances long gone by, had had a share in his life. His gaze followed a bird, a shadow engaged him, the very path, the way it went on and got lost, filled him with a pensive insight, which seemed to him all the purer in that he knew he was independent of it. Where else his dwelling place was would have been a thought beyond him, but that he was only RETURNING to all this, was standing in this body as in the embrasure of a quitted window, looking out and beyond: of this he was a few seconds so convinced, that the sudden appearance of one of his friends in the house would have most cruelly disturbed him, while at the same time he was quite prepared to see Polyxène or Raimondine or some other departed member of the family emerging from the turn of the path . . . In general, he was able to observe how all objects yielded themselves to him more distantly and, at the same time, somehow more truly; this was no doubt due to his vision, which was no longer directed forwards, and which out there, in the open, thinned away; he was looking, over his shoulder, as it were, backwards at things, and that existence of theirs that was closed to him took on a bold, sweet aftertaste, as though everything had been spiced with a trace of the blossom of parting.—Saying to himself from time to time that it could not last, he nevertheless had no fear about the cessation of this extraordinary condition, as though, just as from music, all that was to be expected from it was an

infinitely legitimate close. (Gesammelte Werke, IV, 280 ff. Independent cor-
roboration of the truth, time, and place of this experience is provided by
Princess Marie, *Erinnerungen an Rainer Maria Rilke,* 45–46.)

In 1925 he sent Lou Andreas-Salomé an extract from his note-book which
may be regarded as an addition to the fragment, *Experience,* and which was
probably written at the same time. It begins:

*Later, he thought he could recall certain moments in which the power of
this one was already contained, as in a seed. He remembered the hour in
that other southern garden (Capri), when, both outside and within him,
the cry of a bird was correspondingly present, did not, so to speak, break upon
the barriers of his body, but gathered inner and outer together into one
uninterrupted space, in which, mysteriously protected, only one single spot
of purest, deepest consciousness remained. That time he had shut his eyes,
so as not to be confused in so generous an experience by the contour of his
body, and the infinite passed into him so intimately from every side, that
he could believe he felt the light reposing of the already appearing stars
within his breast.*

He goes on to describe how once, looking through the branches of an
olive tree at the starry sky, he seemed to see the universe face to face. (*Briefe
aus Muzot,* 310–11.) In September, 1912, he and Princess Marie had visited
Saonara, the beautiful villa near Padua belonging to one of her friends.
Two years later, during the dark days of the War, the mention of this name
in one of her letters elicited the following reply: *When you say 'Saonara,'
what a flood of recollection! The things on which formerly no emphasis fell
come to themselves within one,—in me, e.g., a morning hour, early on the
second day, in the little drawing-room next to the billiard-room: no one had
yet come down, I was reading a hymn of some Poeta ignoto . . . and was
full of concentration and pure mental composure. Outside was the park:
everything was in tune with me—one of those hours that are not fashioned
at all, but only, as it were, held in reserve, as though things had drawn to-
gether and left space, a space as undisturbed as the interior of a rose, an
angelical space, in which one keeps quite still. At that time I forgot the
moment, it was in no way decisive for the whole day; it is now present in
me with a peculiar strength and survival, as though made of a higher degree*

of Being. I can think of two, three such moments during the last years (one, beautiful beyond measure, in Cordova—I described it to you [1]); it's as though they sufficed to fill my inner life with a clear, serene splendour, they're such lamps within it, peaceful lamps,—and the more I ponder them in recollection and attentive after-feeling, the more these, according to our present conceptions, content-less experiences seem to me to belong to some higher unity of events. (*Briefe aus den Jahren 1914–1921*, 94–95.)

It was, perhaps, largely through his intense sensibility to such borderline experiences that Rilke reached his characteristic conception of 'the Whole,' and of death as the other, the unilluminated, side of life.

[1] In a letter of December, 1912, quoted in the Introduction to *Requiem and Other Poems*, 66–67; *Briefe aus den Jahren 1907–1914*, 258–59.

Appendix 4

The Task of Transformation

EXTRACT from Rilke's letter of November 13th, 1925, to his Polish translator, Witold von Hulewicz, on the meaning of the *Elegies*.

Transitoriness is everywhere plunging into a profound Being. And therefore all the forms of the here and now are not merely to be used in a time-limited way, but, so far as we can, instated within those superior significances in which we share. NOT, HOWEVER, IN THE CHRISTIAN SENSE (*from which I more and more passionately withdraw*), *but, in a purely mundane, deeply mundane, blissfully mundane consciousness, to instate what is* HERE *seen and touched within the wider, within the widest orbit—that is what is required. Not within a Beyond, whose shadow darkens the earth, but within a whole, within* THE WHOLE. *Nature, the things we move about among and use, are provisional and perishable; but, so long as we are here, they are* OUR *possession and our friendship, sharers in our trouble and gladness, just as they have been the confidants of our ancestors. Therefore, not only must all that is here not be corrupted or degraded, but, just because of that very provisionality they share with us, all these appearances and things should be comprehended by us in a most fervent understanding, and transformed. Transformed? Yes, for our task is to stamp this provisional, perishing earth into ourselves so deeply, so painfully and passionately, that its being may rise again, "invisibly," in us.* WE ARE THE BEES OF THE INVISIBLE. NOUS BUTINONS ÉPERDUMENT LE MIEL DU VISIBLE, POUR L'ACCUMULER DANS LA GRANDE RUCHE D'OR DE L'INVISIBLE. *The "Elegies" show us at this work, this work of the continual conversion of the dear visible and tangible into the invisible vibration and agitation of our own nature, which introduces new vibration-num-*

YANKEE
"MAIN DISH"
CHURCH SUPPER
COOKBOOK

Over 100 kitchen-tested, delicious recipes.

CONTENTS...

INTRODUCTION

The idea for the *Church Supper Cookbook* sprang from a conversation among the editors of *Yankee* magazine. Someone brought up the fact that often the best food in any community was to be found at a local church supper, to which the best cooks in the area are asked to bring "your lasagna," or "that marvelous lemon pie," or whatever their specialty. Another remarked that rarely could one go home and duplicate such a local favorite from a recipe out of a standard cookbook — perhaps, he surmised, because of special touches, or even complete recipes evolved over the years by these culinary experts. The only way to get such a recipe is to ask the cook — "someone should put them in a book. . . . "

Yankee has done just that. We wrote churches all over our region asking for favorite recipes from parish members. The response was staggering — hundreds and hundreds of recipes! These were carefully gone over and selected for originality, taste appeal, and accuracy; those selected were then turned over to the talented and experienced group of cooks who test all recipes published by Yankee. No recipe that did not taste-test *"delicious"* was included. All who took part in the gigantic task of testing the *Church Supper* recipes — many of them church supper cooks themselves — found new and tasty ways to feed their families, as we hope you will.

It is true — many of these can*not* be found in standard cookbooks, but are passed on down through families and friends from generation to generation. The result, here presented, is, we feel, a very special cookbook that will add inspiration and variety to anyone's table.

CONVENTIONS, ABBREVIATIONS, AND EQUIVALENTS

CONVENTIONS

Butter — Wherever butter is called for in a recipe, either butter *or* oleomargarine can be used with equal success. Butter is expensive, oleomargarine more reasonable; there is a slight taste difference — no question, butter *is* better. But if, like the Editor, you have gotten used to margarine, use it by all means.

Flour — Unless otherwise specified in the recipe, "flour" means all-purpose white flour.

Herbs — These are dried unless fresh are specifically required.

Oil, Cooking or Salad — In all recipes except those for Salads, "cooking oil" means liquid corn, safflower, or other vegetable oil, but *not* olive oil. "Salad oil" means your favorite kind — including olive oil.

Shortening — When a recipe calls for *shortening*, solid vegetable shortening such as "Crisco" is meant. Do not use cooking oil, lard, or bacon fat. In a pinch, oleomargarine can be used, as it, too, is solid vegetable shortening, but it is salted, and does have a slightly different taste.

Sour Cream — Where this is called for, the commercial product is meant, not cream soured in your refrigerator.

Spices — These are ground unless whole cloves, crystalline ginger, or stick cinnamon is specified.

Whipped Salad Dressing — A Miracle-Whip-type product.

Sugar — "Sugar" is always white granulated sugar; confectioners' sugar and brown sugar are so specified. Where both brown and white sugars are called for, white granulated sugar is referred to as "white sugar." Brown sugar measurements are for packed amounts.

Baking, Beating, or Blending Times — These may vary slightly with different ovens, beaters, or blenders.

Can Sizes — Sizes vary slightly with different brands, but similar-size cans usually are similar in content. All can sizes given are based on popular brands with national distribution.

Oven Heat — Best results are always achieved by preheating the oven to the temperature required in the recipe. Please read recipe through before you begin to mix ingredients and *preheat oven* to specified temperature.

ABBREVIATIONS

teaspoon(s)..................... t. (1 t. or 2 t.)
tablespoon(s).................. T. (1 T. or 2 T.)
pound(s)...................... lb(s).
ounce(s) .... oz.
package(s) .... pkg(s).
pint(s) .... pt(s).
quart(s)....................... qt(s).
gallon(s) .... gal(s).
degrees Fahrenheit............. °F.
inch(es)....................... " — (9"x13" pan)

EQUIVALENTS

(Courtesy of Shirley T. Oladell, Harwinton Congregational Church, Harwinton, Connecticut.)

pinch or dash .... less than ⅛ teaspoon
3 teaspoons .... 1 tablespoon
2 tablespoons .... 1 liquid ounce
4 tablespoons .... ¼ cup
8 tablespoons .... ½ cup
16 tablespoons .... 1 cup
1 cup .... 1 gill
2 cups .... 1 pint
2 pints .... 1 quart
4 quarts .... 1 gallon
2 cups liquid .... 1 pound
2 cups butter .... 1 pound
2 cups granulated sugar .... 1 pound
4 cups flour .... 1 pound
chocolate, 1 square unsweetened ....1 ounce
4 cups grated cheese .... 1 pound
8 egg whites .... 1 cup (approx.)
16 egg yolks .... 1 cup (approx.)
juice of 1 lemon .... 2-3 tablespoons
1 cup raw macaroni .... 2 cups cooked
1 cup raw rice .... 3-4 cups cooked
1 cup whipping (heavy) cream ...... 2-2½ cups whipped cream

MEATS AND MEAT CASSEROLES

In this chapter, you will find all sorts of exciting ways to serve beef — steak and roasts; meat loaves in interesting and different guises; meatballs to serve with an impressive roster of delicious sauces; ground beef dishes for every occasion, plain or fancy; and several superb stews, which have only beef in common. The Ham, Pork, and Lamb section features equally original and tasty ways to use ham and great casseroles made with pork, lamb, or the humble sausage.

BEEF

ROASTS, STEAKS, AND HASH

ROAST "LION"

The flavors of the two kinds of meat intermingle to create a delicious new taste. Said to be Amish in origin.

Use equal portions of beef and pork roasts, any cut; total weight depends on crowd size. Allow at least ¼ pound per serving, consisting of a slice of each meat. Choose, for example, a beef rump roast and a pork shoulder of approximately the same weight. Place both meats in one roasting pan, cover the pan, and roast as for pork (35 minutes per pound; 45 minutes for rolled, boned pork roast) in a slow (325° F.) oven until done. The beef will be well done, but not dry. Make gravy from the pan juice — the gravy is a most important part of Roast Lion — and serve with noodles or mashed potatoes.

Gayle Flickinger, St. Mark's Episcopal Church, Canton, Ohio

BEEF STROGANOFF

Onion soup mix adds American ingenuity to this Russian classic.

2 lbs. sirloin beef steak cut into
   shoestring strips ½" wide x
   3" long and rolled in flour
2 T. butter
1 4-oz. can mushrooms with
   liquid

3 T. flour
1 envelope onion soup mix
2½ cups water
½ cup sour cream

Brown beef strips in butter. Remove from skillet. Drain mushrooms, reserving liquid, and sauté in drippings in skillet. Remove from skillet. Into drippings stir 3 T. flour and soup mix. Gradually add water and mushroom liquid, blending well and stirring until thickened. Return meat and mushrooms to skillet, cover, and simmer, stirring from time to time, for about 20 minutes, or until meat is tender. Blend in sour cream and serve over hot egg noodles or boiled potatoes. *Serves 6.*

Mrs. Carlos Castro, Harwinton Congregational Church, Harwinton, Connecticut

CHINESE PEPPER STEAK

If you have a pressure cooker, your church will benefit.

2 lbs. boneless beef chuck
2 T. fat
2 large onions, chopped
1½ cups sliced celery
2 cloves garlic, minced
1 t. salt
⅛ t. pepper

2 beef bouillon cubes
1.cup hot water
6 large green peppers, cut in
   eighths
2 T. cornstarch
¼ cup cold water
1 T. soy sauce

Trim fat from beef. Cut in thin strips about 1"x2". Melt fat in pressure cooker. Add meat; cook over direct heat till browned, stirring frequently. Add onions, celery, garlic, seasonings, and bouillon cubes dissolved in hot water. Close cooker, bring to 15-lb. pressure, and process for 3 minutes. Cool (letting pressure go down by itself). Add peppers, simmer for 5 minutes, add cornstarch blended with cold water. Cook till thickened. Add soy sauce. Serve with hot cooked rice or canned chow mein noodles. *Serves 6-8.*

Edie Blackstone, Concord Unitarian Church, Concord, New Hampshire

BEEF STRIPS ORIENTAL

Similar to Chinese pepper steak, but does not need a pressure cooker.

2 lbs. round steak, ¾" thick
2 T. cooking oil or butter
2 cups water (or canned mushroom liquid)
4 T. soy sauce
2 garlic cloves, minced, or ¼ t. garlic powder
2 cups diced celery

1 lb. fresh mushrooms, sliced, or 2 8-oz. cans, drained (see above)
4 T. cornstarch
½ cup cold water
½ cup water chestnuts, sliced
green pepper strips

Cut meat into strips ¼" wide and 3"-4" long. In large heavy saucepan, brown meat on all sides in oil or butter and drain. Add water, soy sauce, and garlic. Cover and simmer 45 minutes over low heat. Add celery and mushrooms, replace cover, and continue cooking for 15-20 minutes longer. Combine cornstarch and cold water, stirring until well blended. Gradually add this to meat mixture, stirring constantly until it boils and thickens. Remove from heat and stir in water chestnuts. Top with pepper strips. Serve over hot rice. *Serves 6-8.*

Ethel Innes, The Unitarian Church, Franklin, New Hampshire

BEEFSTEAK PIE

A good sturdy version of an old favorite.

3 lbs. lean beefsteak cut in 1" cubes
¼ cup butter
¼ cup olive oil
3 T. flour
1 can beef consommé
1 cup dry burgundy
2 medium onions, thinly sliced

1 lb. fresh mushrooms, sliced
1 cup chopped celery and leaves
1½ t. dill weed
1 bay leaf
1 T. Worcestershire sauce
salt and pepper
1 unbaked 9" pie shell
1 T. melted butter

Brown beef in butter and olive oil in large skillet. Sprinkle with flour. Stir in next 9 ingredients. Cover and simmer for 45 minutes. Remove bay leaf. Put into 2-qt. casserole and cover with pie shell. Seal edges with fork, brush with melted butter, and bake at 350°F. for 30 minutes, or until crust is golden brown. *Serves 6-8.*

Rhoda Miller, The Unitarian Church, Franklin, New Hampshire

OLD-FASHIONED BOILED DINNER

A classic dish known outside of New England as "corned beef and cab-bage." Quantities as you like it; schedule given for dinner to be ready at noon.

7:00 A.M. Rinse 4-lb. piece of corned beef in water and place in bottom of large kettle. Cover well with cold water. Add 2 T. sugar, 1 t. pickling spice, and 2 bay leaves. Bring to boiling point and boil 5 minutes. Skim scum off top, turn down heat, and simmer, covered, until tender.

9:30 A.M. Scrub fresh beets within an inch of their lives and add to kettle, leaving skin and a good 4 inches of stem on each beet to prevent bleeding.

10:00 A.M. Add peeled turnips, cut coarsely.

11:00 A.M. Add peeled carrots and onions and a fair-sized cabbage cut in quarters. Add water as necessary to keep liquid level up.

11:30 A.M. Add peeled, cut-up potatoes.

NOON. All should be cooked by now. Peel beets and arrange dinner on one large platter. Serve with hot corn bread or johnnycake, egg gravy (a regular white sauce with 1-2 chopped hard-boiled eggs added), horseradish, and a cruet of vinegar. Apple pie is the perfect dessert.

P. Grimes, First Congregational Church of Pembroke, Pembroke, New Hampshire

RED FLANNEL HASH

If there is any Old-Fashioned Boiled Dinner (above) left over, make this the next day.

Into a skillet put some bacon drippings (use bacon bits too, if desired). Add all the boiled dinner leftovers to this skillet, chop, and mix together. Heat through and serve.

P. Grimes, First Congregational Church of Pembroke, Pembroke, New Hampshire

GLORIFIED HASH

*This versatile dish is good served for breakfast (with hot rolls and fruit),
lunch (with a salad), or supper (with a vegetable). We didn't think one can
of hash could provide six servings. In this recipe, it does!*

1 15-oz. can corned beef hash
1 cup shredded cheese
1 T. flour
¼ t. each of salt and pepper

pinch each of nutmeg and dry
   mustard
2 eggs, beaten
1¼ cups milk

Crumble hash in casserole or 9"x9" pan and sprinkle with cheese.
Mix remaining ingredients and pour over. Bake 35 minutes at
350°F., or until custard is set. Partially cool. *Serves 6.*

Mildred T. Melvin, Concord Unitarian Church, Concord, New Hampshire

MEAT LOAVES

There are almost as many meat loaf recipes as there are cooks, and
certainly even more meat loaf fans. Out of the many submitted, we
picked these four as each being rather special in its own distinctive
way.

APPLE MEAT LOAF

An excellent loaf with a hint of apple-pie taste built right in.

1 large onion, finely chopped
2 T. butter
2½ lbs. ground beef
1½ cups fresh bread crumbs
2 cups finely chopped apples,
   peeled and cored
3 eggs, beaten

1 T. chopped parsley
½ t. pepper
2 t. salt
¼ t. allspice
1 T. prepared mustard, or ¼ t.
   dry mustard
¼ cup catsup

Sauté onion in butter until soft. Then combine all ingredients, mix-
ing thoroughly. Form into loaf and place in 10"x14" baking pan (or
pack into large greased loaf pan). Bake at 350°F. for 1 hour. Remove
from oven and let sit for 15 minutes before serving. *Serves 8-10.*

Evelyn I. Johnson, Our Savior Lutheran Church, Hanover, New Hampshire

BEEF/HAM LOAF WITH MUSTARD SAUCE

A meat loaf with a brand-new taste destined to become an old favorite.

6 slices dry bread or toast
1 lb. ground beef
½ can tomato soup
⅓ cup milk

1 egg
1 medium onion, chopped fine
1 lb. cooked ham, ground

Make bread into crumbs. Combine crumbs with ground beef. Beat together ½ can tomato soup, milk, egg, and onion, and mix with ground beef and crumbs. Add ham, mix well, and pack into 9"x5" loaf pan. Bake 1 hour and 15 minutes at 350°F. Let meat loaf stand 10 minutes after removing from oven. Serve with hot Mustard Sauce (see below). *Serves 8-10.*

MUSTARD SAUCE:
½ can tomato soup
1 egg
1 T. sugar

2 T. prepared mustard
1 T. vinegar
1 T. butter

When loaf is almost done, beat together in mixer all sauce ingredients until well mixed. Pour into saucepan and cook over medium heat, stirring constantly until mixture thickens. Keep warm in double boiler until meat loaf is done.

Jeannette Perron, The Unitarian Church, Peterborough, New Hampshire

BARBECUE MEAT LOAF

The sauce makes the big difference here.

1 onion, minced
1½ T. butter
1½ lbs. ground beef
½ cup fresh bread crumbs
1 egg

½ cup tomato sauce
1½ t. salt
¼ t. pepper

Sauté onion in butter until soft. Combine with other ingredients and mix well. Form into loaf and place in 10"x14" baking pan. Pour ½ cup Barbecue Sauce (see below) over loaf and bake for 1 hour at 350°F., basting from time to time with the remaining sauce. *Serves 6.*

BARBECUE SAUCE:
1½ cups tomato sauce
½ cup water
2 T. vinegar

3 T. brown sugar
2 T. prepared mustard
2 t. Worcestershire sauce

Combine all ingredients in saucepan and heat until well blended, stirring. Use as detailed above to baste meat loaf.

Mona Winn, First Congregational Church, Littleton, New Hampshire

CHEESY MEAT LOAF

Needs no gravy, good hot or cold.

½ cup chopped onion
¼ cup chopped green pepper
1 T. butter
2 lbs. ground beef
1 cup (8-oz. can) tomato sauce
2 eggs, beaten

4 oz. cheddar or American
  cheese, grated
1 cup soft bread crumbs
¼ t. thyme
1 t. salt
½ t. pepper

Sauté onion and green pepper in butter until onion is soft. Remove from heat and mix with other ingredients, blending well. Shape into loaf and place in 10"x14" baking pan, or pack into large greased loaf pan. Bake at 350°F. for 1 hour. *Serves 8-10.*

Terry Lafiosca, The Unitarian Church, Franklin, New Hampshire

MEATBALLS, MEATBALLS, MEATBALLS

You'll find them everywhere — served at church suppers, buffets, family meals, and, yes, dinner parties. Meatballs come in many different guises. Here we have gathered one all-purpose meatball recipe and five different sauces to serve over the meat, each of which imparts its own characteristic flavor, along with three individual recipes just too good to leave out.

MEATBALLS AND GREEN NOODLES

Green noodles add their own colorful touch, but this is just as good with plain egg noodles. Meatballs and sauce can be made the day before and refrigerated, but allow 5-10 minutes longer for baking time. Easily multiplied to serve 12 or 24.

1½ cups soft bread crumbs
½ cup tomato sauce
¾ cup chopped onion
4½ T. shortening
1¼ t. salt
pinch pepper
1 lb. ground beef
¼ cup flour
2 cans consommé

1 cup milk
½ cup grated Parmesan cheese
2 T. tomato paste
⅛ t. garlic powder
4 oz. fresh mushrooms, sliced
    and sautéed in butter, or
    6-oz. can, drained
1 8-oz. pkg. green (or egg)
    noodles

Mix bread crumbs with tomato sauce. Sauté onion in 1½ T. shortening.Mix well. Shape into 2 dozen meatballs 1¼" in diameter. Sauté in 3 T. shortening in skillet until brown on all sides. Remove from skillet while making sauce.

Measure shortening left in skillet and add or pour off until you have ¼ cup in pan. Blend in flour smoothly over low heat. Add consommé and milk, stirring constantly until thickened. Add cheese, tomato paste, garlic, ¼ t. salt, and mushrooms.

Cook noodles according to package directions. In 3-qt. greased casserole dish, place half the noodles, all the meatballs, and ⅓ of the sauce. Then put in rest of the noodles and pour remaining sauce over all. Heat in 350°F. oven for about 20 minutes until bubbling. Serve with additional Parmesan cheese if you like. *Serves 6.*

Flossie H. Ukena, Sherman Congregational Church, Sherman, Connecticut

MAGNIFICENT MEATBALLS

Good-sized meatballs wrapped in crisp bacon with a distinctive sour-cream-and-tomato sauce. May be made ahead and reheated without danger of drying out. Easily doubled or tripled for large groups.

4 lbs. ground beef	1½ t. ground black pepper
4 cups canned tomatoes	1 t. oregano
2 cups fine bread crumbs	1 T. finely chopped onion
2 eggs	24 slices bacon
3½ t. salt	1½ cups sour cream

Mix together beef, 2 cups tomatoes, bread crumbs, eggs, salt, pepper, oregano, and onion. Form into 24 good-sized (about 3″ diameter) meatballs. Wrap each with bacon slice, overlapping bacon carefully. Place meatballs in large flat baking dish (roasting pan is handy) so that overlapped bacon is on bottom. Bake in 350°F. oven for 45 minutes, or until bacon is crisp. Remove from oven and pour off bacon fat. Blend sour cream and remaining 2 cups tomatoes together, pour over meatballs, and return to oven. Turn off heat. Serve with rice when sauce is hot. (To reheat from refrigerated state, put in 275°F. oven for 30-40 minutes.) *Serves 12.*

Elizabeth F. Bauhan, All Saints Church, Peterborough, New Hampshire

BOEUF ABDULLAH
(Lebanese Meatballs)

With its distinctively tart yogurt sauce, this is particularly good served with wheat pilaf.

½ cup chopped onion	1 t. salt
3 T. butter	⅛ t. pepper
1 lb. ground beef	1 cup dry bread crumbs
1 egg, beaten	2 cups plain yogurt
2 slices bread soaked in	
½ cup milk	

Sauté onion in 1 T. butter until transparent. Cool slightly. Mix with meat, egg, bread, and seasonings. Shape into 1¼″ balls and roll them in dry bread crumbs. Brown slowly in remaining 2 T. butter. Drain off all but 2 T. fat. Gently spoon yogurt over and around meatballs. Simmer for 20 minutes. Serve hot with rice or wheat pilaf. For extra flavor dissolve a bouillon cube in the water used to cook the rice. *Serves 6-8.*

First Congregational Church, Littleton, New Hampshire

BASIC MEATBALL RECIPE

This excellent recipe covers just about any need you'll ever have for meatballs!

1½ cups bread crumbs soaked in
    ¾ cup milk or tomato juice,
    or 1½ cups dry stuffing mix
    soaked in 3 cups liquid
2 eggs, beaten
1 large onion, chopped and
    sautéed in 2 T. butter
2 lbs. ground beef, or 1 lb. beef,
    ½ lb. ground pork, and ½ lb.
    ground veal
2 t. salt

¼ t. pepper
butter for sautéeing meatballs
Optional Additions (use only 1
    per batch): 4 T. grated
    Parmesan cheese with 1 T.
    mixed Italian seasoning; 1
    cup applesauce with ½ t.
    nutmeg, mace, or allspice; 2
    T. steak sauce or
    Worcestershire sauce

Mix soaked bread crumbs, eggs, and onion in large bowl. Mixture will be runny. Mix in all the ground meat, salt, pepper, and any optional addition you choose to use. If mixture is too stiff, add a little more liquid until manageable. Roll into small meatballs, using about 1 rounded teaspoon of meat for each Swedish meatball, 1 rounded tablespoon for Italian meatballs. Sauté in large frying pan in butter, turning frequently to brown evenly and to keep them rounded. (It will probably take 3 pansful to use up all the meat. It makes a LOT, but you will be amazed how fast they disappear.) Lift out meatballs carefully when done and do next panful in the same butter, especially if you are going to freeze them.

If you want to freeze them raw, paper plates work well as a base, but be careful not to freeze them in a lump — they'll be almost impossible to get apart. Put the raw meatballs in a bull's-eye pattern on the plate, slip into a freezer bag or cover with transparent wrap, and freeze. Makes 48 small meatballs. *Serves 6 for dinner, 8 for buffet.*

Doris E. Berndtson, Woodmont United Church of Christ, Milford, Connecticut

MEATBALL SAUCES

SOUR CREAM SAUCE:

¼ cup flour	2 cups sour cream
¼ cup melted butter or pan drippings	1 T. dill weed
1 cup water	salt and pepper

Add flour to melted butter or drippings over low heat, blending well until smooth. Gradually add water, stirring, then sour cream and dill, stirring constantly until mixture bubbles and thickens. Do not boil. Season with salt and pepper. Add meatballs and simmer gently until heated through. *Serves 8.*

Kathy Paranya, The Unitarian Church, Franklin, New Hampshire

BROWN SAUCE:

¼ cup butter	2 cups bouillon
¼ cup flour	celery leaves or flakes

Melt butter and blend smoothly with flour. Gradually add bouillon, stirring constantly until smooth. Add several celery leaves or flakes (remove celery before serving). Put in meatballs and simmer gently to heat through. *Serves 6.*

SWEET AND SOUR SAUCE:

1 T. cooking oil	½ cup water
¾ cup pineapple juice	½ cup sugar
2 T. cornstarch	2 slices pineapple, cut in pieces
1 t. soy sauce	1 large green pepper, cut into lengthwise strips
¼ cup vinegar	

Mix oil with pineapple juice and cook over low heat for a few minutes. Mix cornstarch with soy sauce, vinegar, water, and sugar. Add to hot pineapple juice and continue to cook gently, stirring, until juice thickens. Add meatballs, pineapple pieces, and green pepper strips. Simmer all together until meatballs are hot. *Serves 6-8.*

Mrs. Albert F. Porter, Chocorua Community Church, Chocorua, New Hampshire

MUSHROOM SAUCE:

¼ cup minced onion
3 T. cooking oil
3 T. flour

1½ cups chicken broth, or 2
   chicken bouillon cubes
   dissolved in 1½ cups water
1 6-oz. can mushrooms, drained

Sauté onion in oil until golden. Add flour and blend to smooth paste. Gradually add chicken broth, stirring. Cook, stirring, until sauce thickens. Add mushrooms and meatballs and simmer gently until heated through. *Serves 6.*

Barbara Lockhart, United Church of Christ, Keene, New Hampshire

CREAM GRAVY:

3 T. butter
½ cup flour
3 cups beef stock or bouillon

1 cup cream
salt and pepper to taste

Melt butter and add flour, stirring to a golden paste. Add stock gradually, stirring briskly to avoid lumps. Add cream and season to taste. Simmer 4-5 minutes. Add meatballs and let them cook in gravy over low heat for 40 minutes. *Serves 8-10.*

GROUND BEEF CASSEROLES

JACKPOT PIE

A recipe given to a minister's wife by a former missionary to China.

2 lbs. ground beef
1 T. butter
½ cup chopped onion
salt and pepper
2 cans tomato soup
3 cups water

1 8-oz. pkg. egg noodles
2 T. Worcestershire sauce
½ cup sliced stuffed olives
5 cups cream-style corn (2 No. 2
   cans)
1 cup grated cheese

Brown meat in butter. Remove from pan and sauté onion until tender. Add to meat along with salt and pepper to taste, soup, and water. Add uncooked noodles and simmer 10 minutes. Add remaining ingredients and bake 40 minutes at 350° F. *Serves 8.*

Ruth Higgins, Tenney United Methodist Church, Salem, New Hampshire

ITALIAN DELIGHT

Similar to Jackpot Pie, but no corn or olives.

1 lb. ground beef
½ lb. bulk sausage
1 large onion, chopped
pinch garlic
½ t. salt
⅛ t. pepper

1 4-oz. can mushrooms
1 8-oz. pkg. egg noodles
1 can tomato soup
1 6-oz. can tomato paste
1 17-oz. can tomatoes
1 cup grated cheddar cheese

Mix and steam together ground beef, sausage, onion, garlic, salt, and pepper. (To steam, cook 3-5 minutes in covered heavy skillet, until redness disappears from beef.) Do not brown. Add mushrooms and juice. Transfer to greased 2-qt. baking dish. Cook noodles and drain. Add soup, paste, and tomatoes to noodles. Stir well. Add noodles and half the cheese to meat, mixing well. Sprinkle remainder of cheese over top. Bake at 350° F. until casserole bubbles and cheese is melted — 30 minutes. *Serves 6.*

Marcia Fletcher, St. Anne's Episcopal Church, Calais, Maine

BEEF OR PORK CHOW MEIN

A Chinese delight.

1 lb. ground beef or pork
1 medium onion, chopped
2 T. butter
1 t. salt
2 cups diced celery
1 cup water
1 16-oz. can mixed Chinese
vegetables, drained

1 16-oz. can bean sprouts,
drained
1 4-oz. can sliced mushrooms
1 13½-oz. can pineapple tidbits
or chunks, reserve liquid
2 T. cold water
2 T. cornstarch
1 T. soy sauce
¼ cup pineapple liquid

Cook meat and onion in butter until lightly browned. Add salt, celery, and 1 cup water. Bring to boil. Cover and simmer until celery is crisp but soft (about 10 minutes). Add Chinese vegetables, bean sprouts, mushrooms, and pineapple, and heat until hot. Combine cold water and cornstarch. Stir in soy sauce and pineapple liquid and add to meat mixture. Cook until slightly thickened, stirring constantly. Serve hot with cooked rice or chow mein noodles. *Serves 6.*

Carolyn Ramsbotham, St. Thomas More Church, Durham, New Hampshire

SNOWTIME BEEF CASSEROLE

This attractive dish is like a cannelloni without the pasta and the extra effort. Exceptional.

1 lb. ground beef
2 8-oz. cans tomato sauce
¼ cup chopped onion
1 t. dried parsley flakes
½ t. crushed oregano
1 t. crushed basil
¾ t. salt

¼ t. pepper
2 10-oz. pkgs. frozen chopped spinach, cooked and drained
1 pint cottage cheese
1 8-oz. pkg. mozzarella cheese slices

Brown beef in skillet; pour off fat. Stir in tomato sauce, onion, herbs, ½ t. salt, and pepper. Simmer uncovered 10 minutes, stirring occasionally. Combine spinach with cottage cheese and remaining ¼ t. salt. Spoon spinach around edge of baking dish (9"x13"). Pour beef mixture into center. Cut each mozzarella slice into 3 lengthwise strips. Arrange in lattice design over meat. Bake at 375° F. for 20 minutes. *Serves 8.*

Ruth Messer, Concord Unitarian Church, Concord, New Hampshire

TAMALE PIE

A long-time Southwestern favorite.

2 lbs. ground chuck
1 large onion
1 1-lb. can whole tomatoes
1 1-lb. can whole kernel corn, drained
2 T. chili powder

salt and pepper
1 6-oz. can pitted black olives, drained
3 cups milk
2 cups cornmeal
grated cheese

Brown together chuck and onion. Add tomatoes, corn, chili powder, salt and pepper, and simmer for 30 minutes. Remove from heat and add olives. Mix milk with cornmeal and cook until thickened. Line bottom and sides of greased 3-qt. casserole dish with cooked cornmeal mush. Add meat mixture and top with grated cheese. Bake at 325° F. for 30 minutes. *Serves 8.*

Phyllis Shattuck, All Saints Episcopal Church, Pasadena, California

CALORIE COUNTER'S MOUSSAKA

Try this for something ethnic and different. Tastes good warmed up the next day, too. This recipe has 378 calories per serving for 6, or 284 calories for 8.

1 lb. lean ground beef
1 medium onion, chopped
1 large eggplant, peeled and
    cubed (5 cups)
1 8-oz. can tomatoes, cut up
1 1-lb. can mushrooms, drained
¼ cup chopped fresh parsley
1 clove garlic, minced
½ t. oregano

½ t. rosemary, crushed
¼ t. cinnamon
salt and pepper
2 eggs
1 8-oz. pkg. Neufchâtel cheese,
    cut up
1 cup plain yogurt
¼ t. salt

In skillet cook beef and onion until meat is browned. Drain off fat. Stir in vegetables, mushrooms, herbs, and seasonings. Cook, uncovered, for 15 minutes, stirring occasionally. Turn into rectangular baking dish. Use electric mixer or blender to blend together eggs, cheese, yogurt, and ¼ t. salt until smooth. Pour over meat. Bake at 350° F. for 15-20 minutes. *Serves 6-8.*

Dorothea Ruggles, First Congregational Church, Littleton, New Hampshire

CLASSIC LASAGNA PLUS 2

The eggs and zucchini are the two pluses — make the "Total" difference!

1 lb. ground beef
¾ cup chopped onions
2 T. olive oil
1 28-oz. can Italian tomatoes
2 6-oz. cans tomato paste
2 cups water
4 T. chopped parsley
1 t. salt
1 t. garlic powder

½ t. pepper
½ t. oregano leaves
8 oz. lasagna
1 lb. cottage or ricotta cheese
8 oz. mozzarella cheese,
    shredded
1 cup grated Parmesan cheese
3 hard-boiled eggs, sliced
2 cups thinly sliced zucchini

In large heavy pan, lightly brown beef and onion in oil. Then add next 8 items and simmer uncovered about 30 minutes. Meanwhile cook lasagna as directed. In 9"x13" baking pan spread about 1 cup of sauce. Then alternate layers of lasagna, sauce, cottage cheese, mozzarella, Parmesan, hard-boiled eggs, and zucchini, ending with sauce, mozzarella, and Parmesan. Bake at 350° F. for 40-50 minutes until lightly browned and bubbling. *Serves 6-8.*

Sally Hale, Dublin Community Church, Dublin, New Hampshire

CARRY OUT CASSEROLE

A creamy, lasagna-like dish with an unusual fillip — ripe olives.

1 8-oz. pkg. wide egg noodles
2 lbs. ground beef
2 T. butter
2 cups tomato sauce
2 T. flour
2 cups cottage cheese
1 cup sour cream

1 t. salt
½ t. pepper
¼ cup chopped black olives
⅓ cup grated onion
½ cup chopped green pepper
1 T. butter
(grated Parmesan cheese)

Cook noodles according to package directions in boiling salted water. Drain. Brown beef in 2 T. butter. Mix tomato sauce with flour, add to beef, and simmer for 10 minutes. Mix cottage cheese with sour cream, salt and pepper, and olives. Sauté onion and green pepper in 1 T. butter and add to cottage cheese mixture.

Place half the noodles in greased 3-qt. casserole dish. Spread with cottage cheese mixture, top this with remaining noodles, and cover all with beef mixture. Sprinkle, if desired, with grated cheese. Bake at 350° F. for 30-40 minutes or until heated through. *Serves 12.*

Marjorie M. Stultz, Concord Unitarian Church, Concord, New Hampshire

BURGER BUNDLES

One good way to make meat go further.

2 lbs. ground beef
⅔ cup milk
2 cups herb seasoned bread
   stuffing
2 cans condensed cream soup
   (mushroom, celery, or your
   choice)

4 t. Worcestershire sauce
2 T. catsup

Mix beef with milk. Divide into 10 patties. On waxed paper, flatten each patty to form a 6″ circle. Put equal amounts of stuffing in center of each. Draw edges over stuffing and seal. Place in 3-qt. casserole. Combine other ingredients and heat gently until smooth and bubbly. Pour over meat. Bake uncovered at 350°F. for 45-50 minutes. *Serves 10.*

Jill Child, The Unitarian Church, Franklin, New Hampshire

QUICK HAMBURGER AND POTATO CASSEROLE

You can put this one together in a jiffy.

2⅔ cups instant mashed potato flakes

1½ cups sour cream

½ cup water

1 lb. ground beef

3 T. chopped onion, or 1 T. dried minced onion

1 15-oz. can tomato sauce (2 cups)

1 12-oz. can corn (with sweet peppers if you can find it), *un*drained

½ cup water

1 t. salt

¼-½ t. pepper

⅛ t. oregano

½ cup diced American or cheddar cheese

In ungreased 9"x13" baking dish, blend potato flakes with sour cream and ½ cup water. Mixture should be crumbly. If not, add more potato flakes. Pat firmly into bottom of pan. Brown beef (with onions, if using fresh), and add to meat the second ½ cup water and remaining ingredients except cheese. Spoon beef mixture over potatoes. Sprinkle with cheese. Bake at 350° F. for 25-30 minutes. This recipe is easily doubled. *Serves 6.*

Margaret Johnson, Trinity Episcopal Church, Claremont, New Hampshire

ONE DISH MEAL

The title says it all.

1 lb. ground beef

1 cup chopped onion

1 can cream of mushroom soup

2 cups chopped celery

1 cup uncooked rice (not Minute)

1 6-oz. can mushrooms, drained

⅓ cup soy sauce

2 cups boiling water

½ t. salt

¼ t. garlic powder

Brown meat and drain, reserving fat in skillet. Remove meat to 2-qt. baking dish. Sauté onion in reserved fat. Drain off fat and mix onion with meat. Add remaining ingredients and stir to combine. Bake at 350° F. for 1 hour, or until celery is tender. Cover dish for last half hour of baking. *Serves 6.*

Bonnie Ridge, The Unitarian Church, Keene, New Hampshire

BEEF 'N BEAN ROLL-UPS

Children love these. Fun and filling.

¼ cup butter
2 cups flour
2 t. baking powder
½ t. salt
½ cup milk
¼ cup molasses

1½ lbs. ground beef
2 16-oz. cans pork and beans
½ cup chopped onion
½ cup molasses
¼ cup catsup
salt and pepper

Cut butter into dry ingredients. Add milk and ¼ cup molasses, mix well, and form into large ball. Roll out dough on floured surface to 9"x12" rectangle. Brown meat and add to it the remaining ingredients. Bring meat mixture to boil. Spread ¾ cup of meat mixture over rolled-out dough. Starting with 12" side, roll up dough with meat inside and cut the roll into twelve 1" slices. Pour rest of meat mixture into a 9"x13" baking dish and top with dough slices. Bake at 400° F. for 20-25 minutes. *Serves 6-8.*

Janet M. Secchiaroli, First Church of Christ, New London, Connecticut

ARCADIAN SHEPHERD'S PIE

A "souffly" potato topping makes something special out of this Shepherd's Pie.

1½ lbs. ground beef
2 onions, minced
3 T. butter
1 T. tomato catsup
1 t. Worcestershire sauce
salt and pepper to taste
beef stock

2 eggs, separated
½ cup cream
½ cup butter
⅛ t. garlic powder
8-10 potatoes, peeled, boiled, and mashed
grated Parmesan cheese

Brown beef and sauté onions in butter until golden. Mix meat with onions, catsup, Worcestershire, salt and pepper. Add a little meat stock and cook, covered, over low heat for 15-20 minutes. Beat egg yolks until light, whites until stiff. Beat yolks, cream, butter, and garlic powder into mashed potatoes. Gently fold in beaten egg whites. Put meat mixture into casserole and top with potatoes. Sprinkle with Parmesan cheese and bake at 350°F. until puffed and browned. *Serves 6-8.*

BABOOTIE

Exotically and apricotically tasty.

2 lbs. ground beef, or 1 lb.
    ground beef and 1 lb.
    ground pork
2 onions, chopped
1 1-lb. can tomatoes
1½ T. sugar
2 T. curry powder
2 T. vinegar
salt
2 firm bananas, sliced
1 apple, peeled, cored, and diced
1 T. apricot jam, or 4 canned
    apricots, sliced
¼ cup slivered almonds
tomato juice for thinning

Brown meat and drain off fat. Add all other ingredients and simmer gently, stirring frequently, for 30 minutes. Add tomato juice if too thick. Serve over rice. *Serves 8.*

Mary Nichol, First Presbyterian Church, Monroe, New York

SPAGHETTI PIE

Similar to baked lasagna, but less expensive and less effort.

1 8-oz. pkg. spaghetti, broken
    into 2-inch pieces
2 T. butter
⅓ cup grated Parmesan cheese
½ t. salt
¼ t. pepper
1 egg, well beaten
1½ lbs. ground chuck
1 medium onion, chopped
¼ cup chopped green pepper
2 T. vegetable oil
1 jar (15½ oz.) thick spaghetti
    sauce
1 t. sugar
½ t. leaf oregano, crumbled
½ t. garlic salt
1 cup cottage cheese
4 oz. mozzarella cheese,
    shredded

Cook spaghetti in boiling water following label directions; drain. Place in 9"x13" baking dish. Stir in butter, Parmesan cheese, salt, pepper, and egg until thoroughly combined. Spread mixture evenly in pan.

Sauté ground chuck, onion, and green pepper in oil in large skillet until meat is brown; drain. Stir in spaghetti sauce, sugar, oregano, and garlic salt.

Spread cottage cheese over spaghetti layer and top with meat mixture. Bake at 350°F. for 30 minutes. Sprinkle mozzarella cheese over top and bake an additional 10 minutes or until cheese is melted and just begins to brown. Let stand 15 minutes before cutting. *Serves 6.*

Mrs. Thomas E. Denman, Sr., The Congregational Church, East Hampton, Connecticut

PASTITSIO (Greek Macaroni Pie)

This popular recipe happily doubles, triples, quadruples . . . or halves!

1 large onion, finely chopped	¾ t. oregano
2 T. butter or olive oil	2 cups tomato puree
1½ lbs. ground beef	2 T. minced parsley
¾ t. salt	½ lb. small elbow macaroni
freshly ground black pepper	1 T. cooking oil
¼ t. cinnamon	

Sauté onion in butter in large heavy pan or skillet until soft. Stir in ground beef and cook until lightly brown. Season with salt, pepper, cinnamon, and oregano. Stir in tomato puree and parsley. Cover and simmer gently for 20 minutes. Taste, and add more salt if necessary. Cook macaroni in large kettle of well-salted boiling water until tender, but still slightly firm. Drain, then rinse in lukewarm water. Mix oil well through macaroni to prevent it from sticking together. Make Creamy Topping (see below).

CREAMY TOPPING:

3 T. butter	¼ t. nutmeg
3 T. flour	¼ t. salt
3½ cups milk	¼ t. white pepper
3 egg yolks	½ cup Parmesan cheese

Melt butter and blend in flour. Stir in milk and cook about 5 minutes, stirring constantly to make a thin white sauce. Beat egg yolks lightly. Dip out 1 cup of hot sauce and pour in thin stream into yolks, stirring constantly until well blended. Pour mixture back into rest of sauce and stir for a few minutes over low heat. Do not allow to boil. Season with nutmeg, salt, and pepper.

In greased 9"x13" Pyrex casserole, put a thin layer of macaroni, a layer of meat sauce, a second layer of macaroni, and a second layer of meat sauce. Pour Creamy Topping over all. Jiggle the dish so some sauce runs through all layers. Sprinkle Parmesan over top. Bake at 350°F. for 45 minutes. Remove from oven and let stand 15-20 minutes. Cut into large squares and serve from pan. *Serves 8.*

Elizabeth F. Bauhan, All Saints Church, Peterborough, New Hampshire

CANNELLONI

Pasta rolled around a filling of meat, onion, and spinach, doubly sauced red and white. Takes time, but is worth it.

PASTA:

10 lasagna noodles
1 T. olive oil

Add noodles and oil to boiling salted water and cook according to directions on package to just *al dente* stage. Drain and spread noodles side by side on flat area covered with foil. (Noodles will not stick to foil.) Cover with another layer of foil until ready to use.

FILLING:

1 clove garlic, minced
1 large onion, finely chopped
2 T. olive oil
1 10-oz. pkg. frozen spinach,
    thawed, squeezed dry, and
    rechopped
1 lb. ground beef

1 T. butter
5 T. Parmesan cheese
2 T. cream
2 eggs, beaten lightly
½ t. oregano
salt and pepper

Sauté garlic and onion in olive oil until onions are soft. Add spinach to pan and cook, stirring constantly, for 4-5 minutes or until all water has boiled away and spinach shows tendency to stick to pan. Turn into large bowl. Brown meat in butter, turning and stirring to cook evenly and break up all lumps. Add to bowl with spinach, along with Parmesan, cream, eggs, and oregano. Mix well. Salt and pepper to taste.

TOMATO SAUCE:

3-4 cups (24-oz. can) plain
    tomato sauce

BESCIAMELLA (CREAM) SAUCE:

6 T. butter
6 T. flour
1 cup milk

1 cup cream
1 t. salt
⅛ t. pepper

In heavy or enamel saucepan, melt butter over moderate heat. Remove from stove and stir in flour. Return to stove and add milk and cream all at once. Cook, stirring constantly, over medium heat until well blended. Then turn heat up and bring to boil, stirring diligently to prevent sauce from scorching. Turn sauce down and simmer, still stirring, for a minute or more longer until sauce is thick enough to coat the spoon heavily. Remove from heat and add salt and pepper.

ASSEMBLING CANNELLONI:

Pour a thin film of tomato sauce over bottom of 9"x13" baking dish. Cut lasagna noodles exactly in half with sharp knife. Place 1 rounded tablespoon of filling at one end of each lasagna half and roll up. Place in baking dish. You will have three rows of filled halves: the rolls on the two outer rows being lengthwise with longer sides parallel to 13" side of dish; the middle row being placed crosswise, longer sides parallel to 9" side of dish. Dish will contain 16 rolls. (Two extra lasagna noodles were in case any were torn during cooking or handling.) Spread Besciamella Sauce over filled lasagna rolls. Then spoon tomato sauce *over* all; do not mix sauces. Sprinkle with Parmesan and dot with butter. Bake uncovered at 375°F. for 20 minutes, or until bubbling. (Cannelloni may be made ahead, covered tightly with foil or plastic wrap, and refrigerated for a day or two. It will take a little longer to bake a refrigerated cannelloni. For variation, the saucing can be reversed: place rolls on film of tomato sauce as before, but cover rolls first with tomato sauce, and top with cream sauce.) *Serves 6-8.*

BEEF STEWS

COMPANY BEEF RAGOUT

Make sure you have some cheesecloth on hand for the herb bag (bouquet garni) *called for in this succulent stew.*

2 lbs. stew beef, cut in 1" cubes
¼ cup flour
1 t. salt
3 T. fat for browning
3 cups boiling water
2 cups tomato sauce (16-oz. can)
4 sprigs parsley
½ t. marjoram
½ t. thyme
½ t. rosemary

2 bay leaves
1 clove garlic
6 potatoes, cut in pieces
½ cup celery cut in 1" pieces
1 10-oz. pkg. frozen peas
1 T. butter
1 T. sugar
4 small onions, cut in half
4 medium carrots, cut in 1" slices

Shake beef with flour and salt in a paper bag. Brown meat on all sides in fat. Place in 4-qt. dutch oven and cover with water and tomato sauce. Simmer until meat is tender — about 2 hours.

Place herbs and garlic on a square of cheesecloth and draw up edges to make a little bag. Tie tightly at neck with butcher's twine or thread. Add to dutch oven along with potatoes, celery, and peas.

Melt butter with sugar in skillet and add onions and carrots. Cook over medium heat, stirring, until well glazed. Add to meat mixture. Cook until vegetables are tender; check every 30 minutes, though it may take an hour or longer. Remove herb bag. Refrigerate overnight and reheat in oven before serving. *Serves 10-12.*

First Congregational Church, Littleton, New Hampshire

BOEUF BOURGUIGNONNE

Marinating the meat before cooking makes the difference in this version of a favorite French stew.

3 lbs. stew beef, cut into 1½"
  cubes
1 medium onion, sliced
2 cups red wine
1 bay leaf
4 sprigs fresh parsley, or 2 T.
  dried
¼ t. thyme
2 T. cooking oil
½ t. salt

¼ t. pepper
1 carrot, scraped and sliced
1 clove garlic, mashed
3 T. butter
1 T. flour
½ cup consommé
¼ lb. salt pork, diced
24 small white onions
1 cup sliced mushrooms, fresh,
  or canned and drained

Combine the first 11 ingredients in a bowl and let stand for at least 4 hours, turning meat from time to time. Remove meat and pat dry with paper towels. Strain and reserve marinade. Brown meat in 2 T. butter. Add flour and cook 3 minutes, stirring. Add consommé and reserved marinade and bring to boil. Cover, turn down heat, and simmer for 2 hours, stirring from time to time.

Melt remaining 1 T. butter in small saucepan. Add salt pork and onions. Cook over medium heat about 10 minutes, or until golden. Transfer salt pork and onions to stew pot. Add mushrooms. Bring to boil. Cover, turn down heat, and simmer 45 minutes longer, or until meat is tender. Serve with boiled potatoes, noodles, or macaroni. *Serves 8-10.*

Moira Burnham, Church of the Epiphany, New York, New York

LAZY MAN'S BEEF STEW

One of the best, and certainly the easiest. We couldn't believe that "there's no browning of the meat, yet a rich gravy and marvelous flavor develop during the long, slow cooking," and even doubted there would be enough liquid. Doubters no more — we believe!

2 lbs. stew beef
4 large carrots, quartered
    lengthwise and cut into
    pieces
1 can tomato soup
1 bay leaf
3-4 medium potatoes cut into
    quarters

1 cup red cooking wine
2 onions, thinly sliced
1 pkg. frozen peas
(1 cup fresh mushrooms,
    sautéed in butter and
    drained, or 1 6-oz. can,
    drained)

Grease a large casserole dish. Put into it beef, carrots, tomato soup, bay leaf, potatoes, ½ cup wine, and onions. Cover and bake in 275°F. oven for 4 hours. Remove from oven and stir (meat will be a little dry). Add peas (still frozen), optional mushrooms, and remaining ½ cup red wine, and, if necessary, a little water. Cook for 1 hour longer. *Serves 6.*

Ethel Innes, The Unitarian Church, Franklin, New Hampshire

BEEF CHOP SUEY

Like most stews, tastes best made the day before and reheated.

1 lb. stew beef, cut into 1" cubes
1 T. cooking oil
water to cover
5 medium onions, chopped
2 large stalks celery, chopped
1 16-oz. can bean sprouts,
    drained

1 6-oz. can mushrooms with
    liquid
(2 T. diced pimiento)
2 T. (or more) soy sauce
pepper to taste
2 T. cornstarch mixed with ¼
    cup cold water

Brown beef in hot oil in large skillet or 2-qt. dutch oven. Cover with water and simmer until tender — about 2 hours, adding water as needed. Add onions, celery, bean sprouts, and mushrooms, and continue to simmer for 30 minutes more, or until vegetables are tender. Add optional pimiento, soy sauce, and pepper. Stir in cornstarch mixture and cook, stirring, until thickened. Serve over rice or chow mein noodles — do not heat chop suey and rice or noodles together. *Serves 6-8.*

Sharon Rivard, Woodmont United Church of Christ, Milford, Connecticut

BOEUF FLAMANDE

Beef stew in a rich sauce made with beer.

½ lb. salt pork, cut into ¼" cubes
3 lbs. beef stew meat, cut into
   2½" cubes
1 t. salt
½ t. pepper
6 large onions, thinly sliced
1 t. minced garlic
½ cup flour
1½ cups dark beer

2 cups beef or chicken broth, or 2
   bouillon cubes dissolved in 2
   cups boiling water
1 bay leaf
½ t. thyme
2 t. sugar
3 T. wine vinegar
2 T. chopped fresh parsley

Brown salt pork cubes until crisp in large skillet. Lift out to small bowl and reserve. Sprinkle meat with salt and pepper and brown in hot fat over medium heat. Transfer browned meat to 2-quart baking dish or casserole. To fat remaining in skillet (add 3 T. butter if necessary), add the onions and cook gently until golden. Add garlic and cook for 2-3 more minutes. Stir in flour, blending well with onions and garlic and cook for 2-3 minutes. Gradually stir in beer, then broth, stirring constantly over medium heat. Add bay leaf, thyme, and sugar, turn heat to high, and bring to boil. Then turn down heat immediately and simmer sauce for 5 minutes. Pour sauce over meat in casserole, cover casserole, and bake at 375°F. for 1½ hours, or until meat is tender. Stir in vinegar and sprinkle stew with parsley and browned salt pork. Serve over noodles, rice, or boiled potatoes. *Serves 8-10.*

LOUISIANA BEEF STEW

An interesting stew featuring molasses, raisins, and a hint of ginger.

3 T. flour
1 t. salt
½ t. celery salt
¼ t. garlic salt
¼ t. pepper
½ t. ginger
3 lbs. beef chuck, cut in 2" cubes
2 T. cooking oil

1 16-oz. can tomatoes
3 medium onions, sliced
⅓ cup red wine vinegar
½ cup molasses
½ cup water
6-8 carrots, cut on diagonal
½ cup raisins

Combine first 6 ingredients and sprinkle over beef cubes. Brown beef in hot oil. Remove to dutch oven and add tomatoes, onions, vinegar, molasses, and water. Bring to boil, cover, and simmer about 2 hours. Add carrots and raisins and simmer 30 minutes longer, or until carrots are tender. *Serves 8-10.*

Katharine D. Foster, United Church of Christ, Keene, New Hampshire

CHILI CON CARNE

This recipe tastes even better after freezing.

2 lbs. stew beef, cut into ¾"
    cubes
¼ cup cooking oil
1 cup minced onion
2 mashed garlic cloves
2 T. chili powder
1 T. paprika

2 t. oregano
1 t. ground cumin
1 t. salt
¼ t. pepper
1 cup (approx.) water, or 2½
    cups canned tomatoes,
    undrained

Brown beef in oil on all sides. Add onion and garlic and cook 5 minutes, stirring constantly. Stir in seasonings and water or tomatoes. Simmer until meat is tender, from 3 hours to all day (improves with length of cooking time). Stir and add water from time to time to keep liquid at original level. Serve with rice or kidney beans. *Serves 8.*

Mary Nichol, First Presbyterian Church, Monroe, New York

HAM AND PORK

HAM AND CHICKEN LUNCHEON DISH

The naturally delicious combination of ham and chicken is enhanced by just a touch of curry.

¼ cup butter
¼ cup flour
1¼ cups milk
½ cup chicken broth
¼ cup white wine
½ t. curry powder

salt and pepper
1 cup diced cooked chicken
1 cup diced cooked ham
¼ lb. sliced fresh mushrooms, or
    1 4-oz. can, drained
(2 T. diced pimiento)

Melt butter and blend in flour. Add milk and broth gradually, stirring constantly. Bring to a boil, still stirring, and cook until thickened. Lower heat and stir in remaining ingredients one at a time. Simmer 10 minutes, stirring occasionally, until heated through. Serve in patty shells or toast cups or over rice. *Serves 6.*

HAM AND CHEESE ALMOST SOUFFLÉ

Also referred to as a mock soufflé or "strata" casserole, this puffy delight can be made with diced chicken, shrimp, or tuna instead of ham. If you are planning to take one to a potluck supper, bake it at the church, because it will fall slightly as it cools.

8 slices white bread	3½ cups milk
¾ lb. cheddar cheese, cubed	2 t. Worcestershire sauce
3 cups diced cooked ham	1 t. dry mustard
(1 4-oz. can sliced mushrooms, drained)	½ t. paprika
	1 t. salt
6 large or 8 small eggs	⅛ t. pepper

In buttered 3-qt. casserole dish, layer bread, cheese, ham, and optional mushrooms in order given until casserole is full, ending with layer of cheese. Beat together remaining ingredients and pour over casserole. If liquid does not show ⅔ way up in the dish, add more milk. Bake at 350°F. for 1 hour. Serve immediately. *Serves 6-8.*

Women's Association of The Congregational Church, Amherst, New Hampshire

HAM AND RICE DINNER

Ham and rice are the only ingredients you are sure of in this beguilingly different dish. The rest is a guessing game.

3 cups hot cooked rice	1 can cream of chicken soup
2½ cups cooked ham, cut in julienne strips	(2 T. dry white wine)
1½ T. butter	1½ t. prepared mustard
½ cup chopped onion	¼ t. dill weed
2 cups thinly sliced celery	¾ cup sour cream
	⅓ cup sliced pimiento

While rice is cooking, sauté ham in butter for 2 minutes. Add onions and celery and cook over medium heat until tender crisp. Stir in soup, optional wine, mustard, and dill weed, and heat thoroughly. Add sour cream and pimiento. Heat, but do not boil. Serve over hot rice. *Serves 6.*

Diane Gularneau, The Unitarian Church, Franklin, New Hampshire

CRÊPES FASNACLOICH

Crêpes stuffed with ham and chicken and baked in a sherried cream sauce. Easy to make and fabulous to eat. Serve with green salad.

CRÊPES:

2 eggs, beaten
1 cup flour
1 cup milk

1 T. cooking oil
½ t. salt

Put eggs in bowl and beat in flour. Add milk, oil, and salt, beating batter until smooth. Refrigerate to allow ingredients to blend while you make sauce.

SAUCE:

4 T. butter
4 T. flour
3 cups milk
scant ½ t. salt (if you don't use
 salted cooking sherry, use 1
 t. salt)

⅓ cup cooking sherry
(pinch tarragon)

Melt butter in top of double boiler and blend in flour. Add milk, 1 cup at a time, cooking over medium heat and stirring constantly until sauce thickens. Stir in salt, sherry, and optional tarragon. Cover sauce and keep warm over hot water while you cook the crêpes.

Heat 1 T. butter with 1 T. cooking oil on griddle or skillet over high heat until butter is melted and dash of cold water thrown on to griddle bounces in drops rather than sits and boils. Pour off excess fat into measuring cup to leave thin coating on skillet. Turn heat down to medium and ladle batter, a scant ¼ cup at a time, on to griddle. As soon as batter is on griddle, pick up griddle and rotate slowly and smoothly, tilting so that batter spreads evenly to form thin, round pancake 6"-7" in diameter. Return to heat and cook until top side of pancake is just set. Turn (loosen by sliding pancake flipper under, pick up edges of pancake with fingers, and flip). Cook a minute or so on other side (crêpe should be just golden on each side) and stack on plate. Add more of butter-oil mixture if crêpes start to stick. You should have 7-8 crêpes. (This step can be done ahead, as crêpes can be frozen and kept for up to a week.)

MEAT FILLING:

1 cup diced cooked ham
2 cups diced cooked chicken or
    turkey

parsley for final garnish

Mix ham and chicken or turkey together and add ¾ cup sauce, mixing well with meat. Grease 9"x13" baking dish. Place about 2 rounded T. of meat mixture on each crêpe and roll up. Arrange rolled-up crêpes in dish. Pour rest of sauce over filled crêpes and bake at 350°F. for 20-25 minutes (longer if elements of dish are cold to start with), or until sauce is bubbling and filling is heated through. Sprinkle with parsley. *Serves 8.*

O. P. Valhalla, St. Matthew's Church, Bedford, New York

GOVERNOR'S CASSEROLE

The Governor of New Hampshire dropped by for lunch the day this was being tested, and gave it his enthusiastic endorsement.

1 20-oz. pkg. frozen cauliflower
    flowerets
1 20-oz. pkg. frozen broccoli
    flowerets
4 T. butter
3 T. flour
3 cups milk
6 oz. (or 1½ cups) shredded
    cheddar cheese

4 oz. (or 1 cup) grated Parmesan
    cheese
½ t. salt
3 cups chopped ham
3 cups fresh bread crumbs tossed
    with 4 T. melted butter

Cook cauliflower and broccoli in boiling salted water until slightly underdone. Drain and set aside. Melt 4 T. butter in 1-qt. saucepan. Stir in flour and blend well. Gradually add milk, stirring constantly until thickened. Add cheddar, Parmesan, and salt, and stir over low heat until cheese melts. Place vegetables in ungreased 4-qt. casserole dish and sprinkle with chopped ham. Pour cheese sauce over all. Make a border of buttered crumbs around edge of casserole. Bake uncovered at 350°F. for 20-30 minutes, or until crumbs are lightly browned. *Serves 10-12.*

Mrs. Daniel Burnham, Community Church, Dublin, New Hampshire

HAM IN CREAM SAUCE

This versatile recipe can be ladled over English muffins or toast for brunch, served with noodles or rice, or as a side dish with a cheese soufflé.

4 T. butter
4 T. flour
2 cups milk
¼ t. nutmeg
salt and pepper

1 lb. cooked ham, diced
2 t. butter
2 T. chopped chives
6 T. sherry

Melt 4 T. butter in saucepan and add flour, blending well. Add milk, stirring well and cooking over medium heat until thickened. Add nutmeg and salt and pepper to taste. Remove from heat. Cook ham in 2 t. butter about 10 minutes, stirring, and add chives. Cook gently 3-4 more minutes. Add sherry and heat through. Combine the ham with the cream sauce and serve. *Serves 6-8.*

HAM PANCAKE PIE

Sweet potatoes, apples, and ham under an unusual roof.

2 medium sweet potatoes, peeled
    and sliced thinly
3 cups (about ¾ lb.) diced
    cooked ham
3 medium apples, peeled, cored,
    and sliced
½ t. salt
¼ t. pepper

3 T. brown sugar
¼ t. curry powder
⅓ cup water or apple juice
1 cup pancake mix
1 cup milk
½ t. dry mustard
2 T. melted butter

In 2-qt. greased baking dish, layer half the potatoes, half the ham, and half the apples. Combine salt, pepper, brown sugar, and curry powder, and sprinkle half the mixture over layers in dish. Repeat the process with remaining potatoes, ham, apples, and brown sugar mixture. Pour water or apple juice over all. Cover dish and bake at 375°F. until sweet potatoes are tender — about 40 minutes. Beat together pancake mix, milk, mustard, and butter. Take casserole from oven when potatoes are done and pour pancake batter over top. Bake 20 minutes more, uncovered, or until pancake is puffed and golden. *Serves 6.*

HAM LOAF

Ham loaf, like meat loaf, comes in many different guises. Here are three excellent versions. If you have any left over the next day, fry slices lightly in butter for breakfast and serve with omelet or scrambled eggs.

SWEET HAM AND PORK LOAF

1 lb. (4 cups) ground cooked ham	1 cup dry bread or cracker crumbs
⅔-¾ lb. freshly ground raw pork	1½ t. dry mustard
2 eggs, beaten	½ t. salt
1 cup milk	¼ t. pepper

Combine meats and add eggs. Stir in milk, crumbs, mustard, salt, and pepper, and mix well. Form into loaf and place on rack in baking dish, or pack into greased 9"x5" loaf pan. Bake in 400°F. oven until slightly browned (15-20 minutes). Meanwhile, prepare sauce.

SAUCE:

¼ cup vinegar	1 t. prepared mustard, or ½ t.
¼ cup water	dry mustard
¾ cup brown sugar	

Mix all together in saucepan and bring to a gentle boil. Cook for 5 minutes.

Remove loaf from oven and pour over it half the sauce. Return to oven for 30 minutes. At end of this time, pour over rest of sauce; place loaf pan on cookie sheet to catch any sauce that might boil over, and bake for 15 more minutes. When loaf is done, invert pan and remove loaf at once to prevent sticking. *Serves 6-8.*

Shirley T. Oladell, Harwinton Congregational Church, Harwinton, Connecticut

PINEAPPLE UPSIDE-DOWN HAM LOAF

3 T. butter
⅓ cup light brown sugar
canned pineapple slices
(maraschino cherries)
1 lb. (4 cups) ground cooked
   ham
⅔ lb. freshly ground raw pork

2 cups bread crumbs
2 eggs, beaten
1 cup milk
1 t. salt
⅛ t. pepper
½ t. dry mustard

Melt butter with brown sugar and place in bottom of 8"x8"x2" square pan. Place layer of pineapple slices (with a cherry in the middle of each if desired) on top of sugar mixture. Mix together remaining ingredients and spread evenly on top of fruit. Bake at 350°F. for 1½ hours. Turn out on platter and cut into squares. *Serves 6.*

Gladys Delay, Harwinton Congregational Church, Harwinton, Connecticut

HAM LOAF WITH CRANBERRY SAUCE

1 cup milk
1 cup soft bread crumbs (white)
1½ lbs. cured ham, ground

1 lb. fresh lean pork, ground
2 eggs, beaten

Scald the milk and pour it over bread crumbs. Add to meat and mix thoroughly until no bread crumbs show. Add eggs and mix again. Put into 9"x5" loaf pan, then set loaf pan into shallow pan containing hot water at least 1" deep. Bake at 375°F. for 2 hours. If loaf browns too much, cover meat with foil. Pour off fat and excess juice; serve plain or with Cranberry Sauce (see below). *Serves 8.*

CRANBERRY SAUCE:
1 cup canned strained cranberry
   sauce
¼ cup light corn syrup

¼ cup water
whole cranberry sauce for
   garnish

Boil first 3 ingredients until thick. Cool; do not chill. Pour over loaf before serving and put under broiler a few minutes. Garnish platter with whole cranberry sauce. Drain the berries if too juicy.

Nellie H. Crane, The United Church, Northfield, Vermont

FRENCH PORK PIE (Tourtière)

The rich and savory Canadian specialty. Make it as one 10" pie, or as individual meat "pasties" or turnovers.

CRUST:

1 cup shortening　　　　　　　　3 cups flour
1 t. salt　　　　　　　　　　　　⅔ cup water

Cut half the shortening into salted flour, then add remaining ½ cup shortening. Mix well and stir in water. Roll out. Enough pastry for one 10" two-crust pie.

FILLING:

2 lbs. pork, trimmed of fat and　　¼ t. allspice
　　ground or cut into ½" cubes　　2 t. salt
1 lb. ground beef　　　　　　　　½ cup chopped onion
1 cup hot water　　　　　　　　　¼ t. pepper
¼ t. nutmeg　　　　　　　　　　3 cups bread crumbs

Mix all ingredients together, place in pastry-lined 10" pie plate, and top with remaining pastry. Cut a few slits in top crust to allow steam to escape. Bake for 1½ hours at 325°F. or until pie is nicely browned. *Serves 6-8.*

Diane Gularneau, The Unitarian Church, Franklin, New Hampshire

CHICKEN AND TURKEY

Where *would* we all be without these two marvelous birds? Truly they are among the most versatile of all meats — *and* the least expensive. Our talented Church Supper cooks have provided here a marvelous mélange of classics and creations for just about every occasion. None are difficult; all are delicious and all are different.

THE SULTAN'S FAVORITE

An especially nice chicken divan. Goes well with fluffy, hot, buttered rice.

2 broiler/fryers, or a 5-lb. fowl	1 cup milk
2 stalks celery	2 cups strained chicken stock
1 medium onion	1 t. curry powder
salt	1 t. lemon juice
2½ cups water	1 cup mayonnaise
6 T. butter	2 10-oz. pkgs. frozen broccoli
½ cup flour	pimiento strips

Simmer chicken with celery and onion in lightly salted water until tender. Remove meat from bones in large pieces. Strain and reserve stock. Melt butter in saucepan, blend in flour, and gradually add milk and stock. Cook over low heat until thick and smooth, stirring constantly. Remove from heat and add curry powder, lemon juice, and mayonnaise. Beat with rotary beater until very smooth. Cook and drain broccoli. Arrange in bottom of greased 3-qt. casserole. Place pieces of chicken on top and pour sauce over all. Garnish with pimiento strips and bake at 400° F. for 20 minutes or until heated through. *Serves 8.*

Baptist Women's Fellowship, New London, New Hampshire

CHICKEN ORIENTAL

An interesting combination of tastes and textures. Serve with extra soy sauce on the side.

1 10-oz. pkg. frozen peas
1 cup diced cabbage
1 5-oz. can water chestnuts,
    drained
¼ cup cooking oil
6 T. flour
½ t. ground ginger
2½ cups chicken stock
1 T. soy sauce

2 cups cooked, diced chicken
1 4-oz. can sliced mushrooms,
    drained
1 5-oz. can bamboo shoots,
    drained
1 16-oz. can mixed Chinese
    vegetables, or 2 cups fresh
    bean sprouts

Boil peas and cabbage together 2 or 3 minutes until crisp. Slice water chestnuts. In large skillet, heat oil, blend in flour and ginger, and stir until smooth. Add chicken stock slowly, stirring constantly until sauce thickens and bubbles. Add soy sauce, chicken, peas and cabbage, mushrooms, shoots, and Chinese vegetables. Stir thoroughly until hot. Serve over hot rice or noodles. *Serves 6-8.*

Betty W. Doyle, United Church of Christ, Keene, New Hampshire

LAYERED CHICKEN

If you freeze this casserole, do not add the Chinese noodles until ready to bake.

1 "three legged" chicken, cooked
1 can cream of mushroom soup
1½ cups cooked rice
2 4-oz. cans mushroom pieces,
    or ½ lb. fresh, sliced

1 pt. sour cream
½ pkg. dry onion soup mix,
    crushed
1 5-oz. can chow mein noodles

Cut chicken meat from bones into large pieces. Place in bottom of greased 2-qt. baking dish. Pour over mushroom soup. Add a layer of rice and a layer of mushrooms. Pour sour cream over all and sprinkle with onion soup mix. Cover with chow mein noodles and bake at 350° F. until hot and bubbly. *Serves 6.*

Charlotte Stone, First Congregational Church, Portland, Connecticut

CHICKEN PIQUANT

Chicken pieces cooked in spicy white-wine sauce.

1 broiler/fryer cut up into 6-8
    pieces
¾ cup white wine
¼ t. salt
¼ cup cooking oil

2 t. ground ginger
¼ t. oregano
¼ cup soy sauce
1 cup chicken broth
2 T. brown sugar

Place chicken pieces in dutch oven. Combine remaining ingredients and pour over chicken. Cover and bake at 375° F. for 1 hour. Then uncover and bake at 400° F. for 15 minutes more to brown and thicken sauce. Serve with rice. *Serves 6.*

Jill Child, The Unitarian Church, Franklin, New Hampshire

LAZY CHICKEN IN HERBED SAUCE

A Hollandaise-like sauce that makes itself. Cook a package of frozen broccoli right along and in with 1 cup raw rice, and serve chicken and sauce with or over this Broccoli-Rice.

1 broiler/fryer, cut into 6-8
    pieces
2 T. butter
2 T. cooking oil
1 t. grated lemon rind

¼ t. each of basil and oregano
2 T. lemon juice
1 can cream of chicken or cream
    of mushroom soup

Skin chicken and brown lightly in hot butter and oil. Drain off fat and place chicken in baking dish. Mix lemon rind, herbs, lemon juice, and soup together and spoon over top of chicken. Cover and bake at 325° F. for 1-1¼ hours. Can be made the night before and reheated. *Serves 6.*

Evelyn H. Chase, Concord Unitarian Church, Concord, New Hampshire

SPRING CHICKEN MARYLAND

A specialty of dining-car chefs during the Golden Age of Pullman travel that well deserves its fame. Easily divided.

3 broiler/fryers, cut up
6 T. cooking oil
¼ cup flour
½ t. salt
⅛ t. pepper
3 slices salt pork ½" thick, cut in
   square dice

3 pinches nutmeg
¾ cup melted butter
3 cups cream or evaporated milk
paprika
parsley sprigs for garnish

Cut chickens into quarters. Brush with oil and dredge with flour, salt, and pepper. Fry salt pork until brown. Add nutmeg. Place chicken on top of pork (without draining off fat) and baste with melted butter. Cover skillet and cook about 30 minutes over medium-low heat until tender. Turn chicken pieces over. Add 1 cup cream, turn heat up to medium, and cook uncovered to let cream cook down. When sauce is fairly thick, add another cup cream, cook as before until thickened, and add the last cup cream. Cook until thick. To serve, spoon cream gravy over chicken pieces, sprinkle with paprika, and garnish with parsley sprigs. *Serves 12.*

HOT CHICKEN SALAD

Crunchy and flavorful chicken dish. For variety, substitute ½ cup diced onion and ½ cup diced green pepper for 1 of the 2 cups of celery.

2 cups cubed cooked chicken
2 cups thinly sliced celery
1 cup mayonnaise
½ cup toasted slivered almonds
2 t. lemon juice

½ t. salt
½ cup grated cheese
1 cup toasted bread cubes or
   croutons

Combine all ingredients except the cheese and bread cubes. Pile lightly into greased baking dish. Sprinkle with bread cubes and cheese. Bake at 450° F. for 20 minutes, or until bubbly. *Serves 6.*

Shirley T. Oladell, Harwinton Congregational Church, Harwinton, Connecticut

CHICKEN PIE

A dish you can't go wrong with is Chicken Pie; whether you make it with biscuit or pie-crust topping, everybody likes it. Here's how both ways.

CHICKEN PIE WITH CRUST

2 cut-up broiler/fryers
1 large onion, quartered
4 carrots, scraped and cut into
  pieces
2-3 cups water
¼ t. rosemary
½ t. thyme

¼ t. marjoram
2 t. salt
1 t. pepper
1 10-oz. pkg. frozen peas
⅓ cup butter
⅓ cup flour
1 cup cream

Put chicken into pot with onion and carrots. Add water to cover, rosemary, thyme, marjoram, 1 t. salt, and ½ t. pepper. Bring to boil and simmer, covered, for about 45 minutes or until chicken is cooked. Drain chicken and reserve broth. Remove bones and skin from chicken pieces and cut meat into bite-sized chunks. Return chicken to vegetables and add frozen peas. Remove 1½ cups broth from pot. Melt butter in saucepan and blend in flour. Gradually add hot broth and cream, stirring constantly until thickened and smooth. Add remaining 1 t. salt and ½ t. pepper. Pour sauce over chicken and vegetables, adding more broth if necessary.

PASTRY:

1 cup shortening
3 cups flour

½ t. salt
½-¾ cup cold water

Cut shortening into flour mixed with salt. Add water. Mix well to form ball. Roll out top and bottom crusts.

Place bottom crust in 9" deep-dish pie plate. Pour in chicken mixture and cover with top crust. Brush with milk. Pierce three small holes in top crust to let steam escape and put ring of foil around edge to prevent over-browning. Bake at 350°F. for 35-40 minutes, or until brown, removing tinfoil after about 10 minutes. *Serves 6-8.*

Crust: Evelyn Shaw, Pilgrim Congregational Church, New Haven, Connecticut

CHICKEN PIE WITH BISCUIT TOPPING

Use the recipe on p. 44 for chicken, vegetables and sauce. Place in 9"x13" baking dish and top with Baking Powder Biscuits.

BAKING POWDER BISCUITS:
2 cups flour
4 t. baking powder
1 t. salt

⅓ cup shortening
¾ cup milk

Sift together dry ingredients and cut in shortening. Add milk to make soft dough. Knead a few times on floured board. Lightly roll out to ½" thickness and cut with 2" cutter. Bake at 450°F. for 10-15 minutes until chicken mixture is hot and biscuits are well browned. *Serves 6-8.*

Biscuits: Susie Cleveland, The United Church, Northfield, Vermont

NUTTY CHICKEN PIE

Chicken, mushrooms, and almonds in a velvety cream sauce under a pastry cover.

¼ cup butter
¼ cup flour
1 cup light cream
½ t. salt (omit if you use bouillon cube to make broth)
¼ t. pepper
1 cup chicken broth

¼ t. dill weed
1 t. chopped parsley
2 cups cooked diced chicken
1 4-oz. can sliced mushrooms, drained
½ cup toasted slivered almonds
pastry for single-crust 9" pie

Melt butter and blend in flour. Gradually stir in cream, and cook, stirring, until smooth and thick. Add salt, pepper, chicken broth, dill weed, and parsley, and cook until once more smooth and thick. Stir in chicken, mushrooms, and almonds. Pour into deep 9" pie plate and cover with pastry. Slash top and bake on cookie sheet in oven preheated to 450°F. for 10 minutes. Reduce heat to 350°F. and bake 15 minutes more. *Serves 6.*

CHICKEN RICE CASSEROLE

An elegant version of a hot chicken salad.

2 cups diced cooked chicken
1 cup sliced celery
2 t. finely chopped onion
½ cup chopped walnut meats
2 cups cooked rice
1 can cream of chicken soup
½ t. salt

¼ t. pepper
1 T. lemon juice
½ cup mayonnaise
½ cup water
3 hard-boiled eggs, sliced
2 cups crushed potato chips

In large bowl, combine first 9 ingredients. Mix mayonnaise with water until smooth and add to chicken mixture. Gently fold in egg slices. Turn mixture into greased 9" square pan. Bake at 450°F. for 25 minutes. Remove, and top with potato chips. Return to oven for another 5 minutes. *Serves 6-8.*

Emilie C. Bugbee, The Congregational Church, Somers, Connecticut

RICH CHICKEN NOODLE CASSEROLE

Tabasco lends a special touch to this creamy invention.

3 cups uncooked medium egg
    noodles
1 cup cottage cheese
1 cup sour cream
6 T. grated Parmesan cheese

1½ t. salt
¼ t. Tabasco sauce
¼ cup sliced pitted ripe olives
2½ cups diced cooked chicken

Cook noodles according to package directions. Combine cottage cheese, sour cream, 4 T. Parmesan, salt, and Tabasco. Stir in olives, noodles, and chicken. Turn into greased 2-qt. casserole and sprinkle with remaining Parmesan cheese. Cover and refrigerate. One hour before serving, place in 350°F. oven and bake, covered, for 35 minutes. Uncover and bake for 25 minutes longer. *Serves 6.*

Woodmont United Church of Christ, Milford, Connecticut

PEACHY CHICKEN

A fruitful combination of flavors; good served over rice.

3 chicken breasts, halved
½ cup flour
salt and pepper
2 T. butter
2 T. cooking oil
1½ cups orange juice

2 T. vinegar
2 T. brown sugar
1 t. basil
½ t. nutmeg
1 16-oz. can peach (or apricot)
   halves, drained

Shake chicken pieces in bag with flour and salt and pepper; brown in butter and oil. Place browned chicken in greased 3-qt. casserole dish. Combine orange juice with vinegar, sugar, basil, and nutmeg, and pour mixture over chicken. Cover and bake at 375°F. for 1 hour and 15 minutes, or until tender. Baste often. Then place peach or apricot halves between chicken pieces, baste well, and bake uncovered for 15 minutes longer. *Serves 6.*

Barbara Pasichuke, First Congregational Church, Littleton, New Hampshire

CHICKEN SOUFFLÉ

This recipe has been multiplied to serve over a hundred for a church luncheon or dinner. Just as good warmed up.

16 slices white bread, buttered
   on one side, with crusts
   removed
3-4 whole chicken breasts,
   cooked, boned, skinned, and
   sliced
½ cup mayonnaise

1 cup grated cheddar cheese
5 eggs
2 cups milk
1 t. salt
1 can cream of mushroom or
   cream of chicken soup

Butter a 9"x13" baking dish. Line bottom with 8 slices bread. Cover with sliced chicken meat, spread slices with mayonnaise, and sprinkle with ½ cup cheddar cheese. Top with remaining 8 slices bread. Beat together eggs, milk, and salt, and pour over entire casserole. Refrigerate overnight or all day. When ready to bake, spread soup over top. Bake at 350°F. for 45 minutes. Sprinkle with remaining ½ cup cheddar cheese, return to oven, and bake for 15 minutes longer. *Serves 10.*

Joan Dean, Grace Congregational Church, Rutland, Vermont

CHICKEN À LA KING

This used to be THE dish for special occasions, but somehow you don't run into it as often these days. Still good, though.

1 cup sliced mushrooms
4 T. butter
4 T. flour
½ t. salt
¼ t. pepper

2 cups milk or chicken stock
2½ cups cooked diced chicken
1 cup cooked peas
3 T. diced pimiento

Sauté mushrooms in butter. Blend in flour, salt, and pepper. Gradually stir in milk or stock. Cook over medium heat, stirring, until thickened. Add chicken, peas, and pimiento. Heat well and serve in patty shells or Toast Cups (see below). *Serves 8.*

TOAST CUPS:
Cut crusts from bread slices. Press slices into muffin tins so four points of bread stick up. Bake at 400°F. about 10 minutes or until toasted and brown. Allow to cool a few minutes in pan so cups will hold their shape. If making these ahead, warm them for a few minutes on a cookie sheet before using.

CHICKEN POTATO CASSEROLE

Thyme-touched scalloped potatoes topped and cooked with chicken.

4 cups thinly sliced peeled
   potatoes
4-5 medium onions, sliced
salt and pepper
ground thyme
½ cup hot water

1 13-oz. can evaporated milk
2 slices bacon
2 T. butter
2 broiler/fryers, about 3 lbs.
   each, cut up

Put potatoes and onions in large roasting pan and sprinkle with seasonings. Add hot water. Reserve ¼ cup milk and pour remainder over vegetables. Put in hot oven (400°F.) while preparing chicken.

In large skillet, cook bacon until browned; remove and drain. Add butter to skillet, then chicken, and brown on all sides, removing pieces as they brown. Put chicken in pan with potatoes and sprinkle lightly with salt, pepper, and thyme. Crumble bacon and sprinkle over top. Cover tightly with foil and bake at 400°F. 1 hour. Uncover, pour reserved milk over top, and sprinkle with paprika. Bake 30 minutes longer. *Serves 8.*

Don Wyant, Woodmont United Church of Christ, Milford, Connecticut

CHICKEN LOAF OR RING

Like its first cousin, meat loaf, good cold or hot. Fill a hot chicken ring with rice or macaroni, a cold ring with fresh salad.

2 cups scalded milk	1 t. Worcestershire sauce
2 eggs, lightly beaten	3 cups diced cooked chicken
1 cup soft bread crumbs	½ cup chopped celery
½ t. salt	1 green pepper, chopped
¼ t. paprika	1½ T. lemon juice

Pour hot milk slowly in a thin stream on to eggs, stirring constantly. Add remaining ingredients, mix well, and pour into buttered loaf pan or ring mold. Bake at 300°F. until knife inserted in center comes out clean — 45-60 minutes, approximately. The ring will cook in less time than the loaf. Do not overbake. Remove from oven and let stand 10 minutes before unmolding. *Serves 6-8.*

CHICKEN SPAGHETTI DINNER

Spaghetti with a difference. The secret is the long simmer.

1 green pepper, chopped	1 broiler/fryer cut up, or 3 large
1 cup diced celery	chicken breasts, halved
2 large onions, chopped	1 t. cinnamon
3 cloves garlic, chopped	1 t. salt
½ cup cooking oil	½ t. pepper
1 16-oz. can tomato puree	½ t. allspice
2 6-oz. cans tomato paste	1 8-oz. pkg. spaghetti
2 puree cans water	

Sauté green pepper, celery, onions, and garlic in ¼ cup cooking oil. Add tomato puree, paste, and water. Simmer 1½ hours, uncovered, stirring from time to time. Brown chicken pieces in remaining ¼ cup oil. Add with cinnamon, salt, pepper, and allspice to simmering sauce and continue to simmer, covered, for 1½ hours longer, or until chicken is tender. Cook spaghetti as directed and drain. Place in serving dish. Pour chicken and sauce over spaghetti. *Serves 6.*

Virginia Colivos, Greek Orthodox Church of the Annunciation, Dover, New Hampshire

CHICKEN SOUR CREAM BAKE

Rich, different, and distinguished — but, oh, so easy to do. The chipped beef ends up tasting like Italian prosciutto ham.

6 chicken breast halves, skinned, boned, and halved again if too large to be wrapped in beef slice
1 4-oz. jar chipped beef, rinsed in boiling water and drained
12 slices bacon
2 cups sour cream
1 can cream of asparagus or cream of mushroom soup
paprika

Wrap each breast section in slice of chipped beef, then wrap with bacon. Mix sour cream and soup. Place chicken in greased casserole dish and pour soup mixture over it. Sprinkle with paprika. Bake uncovered at 325° F. for 2 hours. *Serves 6-8.*

Catherine B. Anderson, United Methodist Church of the Hamptons, Hampton, New Hampshire

CALIFORNIA OVEN-FRIED CHICKEN

Moist, tender, and habit-forming!

1 frying chicken, cut into 8 pieces
¼ lb. melted butter
⅛ t. garlic powder
⅛ t. paprika
⅛ t. thyme
1 t. salt
1½ cups dry bread crumbs or finely crushed cornflakes

Dip chicken pieces in butter, then shake in paper bag containing seasonings and crumbs or cornflakes. Place skin side up in lightly greased 9"x13" baking dish and bake 50 minutes at 350°F., or until done. *Serves 6-8.*

Mary Wakefield, First Congregational Church, Rindge, New Hampshire

MANICOTTI WITH CREAMED CHICKEN AND ALMONDS

Easier to make than it appears, and very elegant.

12 manicotti*
1 chicken, cooked, skinned, boned, and cut into ½" cubes
1 T. dry white vermouth
½ lemon
1½ T. butter
¼ cup finely chopped onion
2 T. flour
1 cup chicken broth
½ cup heavy cream

½ cup grated Gruyère or Swiss cheese
salt and freshly ground pepper
1 t. butter
3 T. blanched almonds
1 small egg
1 cup ricotta cheese
6 T. Parmesan cheese
3 T. chopped parsley
½ t. grated lemon rind

Cook manicotti according to package directions; set aside on tinfoil and spread out so that manicotti do not stick together.

Place chicken in bowl with vermouth and squeeze lemon over meat. Sprinkle with salt and pepper and set aside.

Melt 1½ T. butter in saucepan and add onion. Cook, stirring, until onion is wilted. Sprinkle with flour and cook, stirring with wire whisk or fork. Add broth, stirring rapidly with whisk. When thickened and smooth, add ¼ cup cream. Simmer about 10 minutes, stirring occasionally; then add Gruyère cheese and salt and pepper to taste. Stir to blend and set aside.

Meanwhile, melt 1 t. butter in small skillet and add almonds in one layer. Place in 350° F. oven and bake until golden brown, shaking the skillet and stirring the almonds from time to time so they won't burn. Remove and let cool. Add cheese sauce and almonds to chicken, along with remaining heavy cream, egg (if the egg is large, beat, measure, and use only half), ricotta cheese, 4 T. Parmesan, and chopped parsley. Blend well with fork or whisk.

To assemble, spoon equal amounts of chicken mixture down center of each manicotti and roll up to enclose filling. In baking dish large enough to hold rolled manicotti in one layer, spoon enough sauce into dish to cover bottom. Arrange filled manicotti over sauce and cover with remaining sauce. Bake, covered, for 30-40 minutes at 350° F. until piping hot and bubbling. Sprinkle with remaining 2 T. Parmesan cheese and run briefly under the broiler to glaze. Sprinkle with grated lemon rind and serve hot. *Serves 10-12.*

Helen D. Tawse, St. James' Episcopal Church, Keene, New Hampshire

*Lasagna noodles may be substituted for manicotti. Use as described under "Cannelloni," p. 26. Crêpes (p. 34) can also be used.

VEGETABLE DISHES AND CASSEROLES

Vegetarians aside, most of us expend our energy fixing an entrée of meat, poultry, or fish, and allot only a few minutes of cooking time to heat up a package of frozen vegetables on the side. But sometimes, when the garden is in full fling, a vegetarian friend comes to dine, or you are asked to contribute a casserole for a Lenten potluck supper, it's fun to spend a little more time on just vegetables.

Vegetable casseroles are not only made to order for all these situations, but are also interesting enough in their own right to consider building a meal around. With fresh bread, rolls, or biscuits, a good change of pace; or serve a vegetable hot dish with a platter of sliced cold meat or cheese.

BAKED APPLE AND CARROT CASSEROLE

A perfect companion for baked beans, ham, or pork.

6 apples, cored, peeled, and
   thinly sliced
2 cups cooked carrot slices
⅓ cup brown sugar

2 T. flour
salt to taste
¾ cup orange juice

Place half the apples in greased 2-qt. baking dish and cover with half the carrots. Mix brown sugar, flour, and salt and sprinkle half the mixture over the carrots. Repeat layers and pour orange juice over top. Bake at 350°F. for 45 minutes. *Serves 6.*

Alma L. Hedrick, Harwinton Congregational Church, Harwinton, Connecticut

ORANGEY BEETS

Similar to Harvard Beets, but uses orange juice instead of vinegar.

1½ T. butter	2 T. grated orange rind, divided
⅓ cup brown sugar	3 cups diced, cooked beets, or
1½ t. cornstarch	canned, drained
⅔ cup orange juice	4 shakes each salt and pepper

Melt butter. Mix sugar and cornstarch, stir into butter. Stir in orange juice gradually and cook, stirring constantly, until thickened. Blend in 1 T. orange rind and beets. Shake over salt and pepper, and remaining 1 T. orange rind. *Serves 8.*

Mary Wakefield, First Congregational Church, Rindge, New Hampshire

BROCCOLI CASSEROLE

Serve as a main dish, or halve to serve 8 as a side dish.

2 10-oz. pkgs. frozen broccoli	pepper to taste
1 can cream of mushroom soup	4 T. chopped onion
1 cup mayonnaise	crushed Ritz crackers for
2 eggs, beaten	topping
1 cup grated sharp cheese	4 T. butter

Cook broccoli for 5 minutes in boiling salted water. Drain well. Combine soup, mayonnaise, eggs, cheese, pepper, and onion. Mix well. Add broccoli and turn into greased 2-qt. baking dish, sprinkle with crushed Ritz crackers, and dot with butter. Bake at 350°F. for 30 minutes until it bubbles and browns. *Serves 8.*

Kate Barnes, St. Paul's Episcopal Church, Fort Fairfield, Maine

BROCCOLI AND CHEESE CASSEROLE

An unusual casserole a little like a soufflé, but not as fluffy.

3 eggs	2 t. salt
1 cup cottage cheese	dash pepper
½ cup cheddar cheese	2 10-oz. pkgs. frozen broccoli
3 T. flour	

Beat eggs, then stir in other ingredients except broccoli and beat well together. Cook broccoli as directed and drain well. Add to egg mixture. Pour into greased baking dish and bake at 350°F. for 30-35 minutes. *Serves 6-8.*

Betty Fainelli, Harwinton Congregational Church, Harwinton, Connecticut

STUFFED BROCCOLI

Creamed broccoli with crunch and crumbs.

2 10-oz. pkgs. frozen chopped
   broccoli
4 T. butter

4 T. flour
2 chicken bouillon cubes
2 cups milk

Cook broccoli according to package directions. Drain and set aside. Melt 4 T. butter, add flour and mix. Add bouillon cubes and milk. Cook until sauce thickens. Grease a 2-qt. baking dish and place broccoli in it. Pour sauce over.

TOPPING:

2 cups seasoned stuffing mix
6 T. butter

⅔ cup water
⅔ cup chopped walnuts

Mix seasoned stuffing mix with butter, water, and chopped walnuts. Place on top of sauce and bake 20-30 minutes at 350°F. *Serves 6-8.*

Lina Storrs, Center Congregational Church, Torrington, Connecticut

CARROT CASSEROLE

Carrots enlivened with onion and horseradish. Fix ahead and heat when ready.

2 bunches (2 lbs.) carrots
½ cup carrot liquid
4 T. grated onion
1½ t. horseradish
½ cup mayonnaise

1 t. salt
¼ t. pepper
1 cup dry bread crumbs
½ cup melted butter

Scrape, dice, and boil carrots in salted water until crisply done. Drain, reserving ½ cup liquid. Place in greased 2-qt. casserole. In small bowl mix carrot liquid, onion, horseradish, mayonnaise, salt, and pepper. Pour over carrots. Top with bread crumbs and pour melted butter over all. Bake at 375°F. about 20 minutes or until slightly brown and bubbly. *Serves 6.*

Shirley T. Oladell, Harwinton Congregational Church, Harwinton, Connecticut

CARROTS EXCELSIOR

Colorful and custardy.

2½ cups carrots, cooked,
    mashed, and seasoned with
    salt and pepper
2 egg yolks, beaten

1½ cups milk
1 cup bread crumbs
1 T. finely chopped onion
2 egg whites

Mix all, except egg whites. Beat egg whites stiff and fold lightly into carrot mixture. Turn into buttered 1½-qt. casserole. Bake at 350°F. for 45-60 minutes, or until knife inserted comes out clean. Serve hot. *Serves 6-8.*

Mrs. Albert G. Clark, United Church of Christ, Keene, New Hampshire

FAR EAST CELERY

Delicious served with steak or chicken.

4 cups celery, cut in 1" pieces
1 5-oz. can water chestnuts,
    drained and sliced
1 can cream of chicken soup
1 small jar pimiento, drained
    and chopped

2 T. butter
½ cup slivered almonds
½ cup bread crumbs

Cook celery in small amount of boiling salted water for about 8 minutes. Drain. In buttered 1-qt. casserole, mix celery, water chestnuts, soup, and pimiento.

Melt butter in skillet and lightly brown almonds. Add bread crumbs and sprinkle mixture over casserole. Bake in 350°F. oven for 35 minutes. *Serves 6.*

CORN-ZUCCHINI BAKE

A nice combination. Try also topped with tomato sauce.

3-4 medium (1 lb.) zucchini
¼ cup chopped onion
1 T. melted butter
2 eggs, beaten
2 T. flour
1 10-oz. pkg. frozen whole
    kernel corn, or 2 cups fresh
    corn cut from cob, cooked
    and drained
1 cup (4 oz.) shredded Swiss
    cheese

¼ t. salt
¼ cup fine dry bread crumbs
(1 t. oregano or Italian
    seasoning)
2 T. grated Parmesan cheese
1 T. melted butter
tomato halves
parsley

Wash zucchini; do not pare. Slice about 1" thick. Cook, covered, in small amount boiling salted water until tender (15-20 minutes). Drain and mash with fork. Sauté onion in 1 T. melted butter until tender. Combine beaten eggs, flour, mashed zucchini, onion, corn, Swiss cheese, and salt. Turn into greased 1-qt. casserole or 7" square baking dish. Combine bread crumbs, oregano or Italian seasoning if desired, and Parmesan cheese with 1 T. melted butter. Sprinkle over corn mixture. Place on baking sheet. Bake at 350°F. for 40 minutes if using 1-qt. casserole, or for 25-30 minutes if using square baking dish — or until knife inserted comes out clean. Let stand 5-10 minutes before serving. Garnish with tomato halves and parsley. *Serves 6.*

Mrs. L. Bouchard, St. Paul's Church, Lancaster, New Hampshire

EGGPLANT CASSEROLE

For a different note at a potluck supper.

½ can golden mushroom soup
½ cup mayonnaise
1 egg, beaten
1 T. grated onion
1 cup shredded cheese

1 medium eggplant, peeled,
    diced, and cooked in boiling
    salted water for 10-15
    minutes
¾ cup crushed Ritz crackers
    (about 15 crackers)
1 T. butter

Mix soup, mayonnaise, egg, onion, and cheese with eggplant. Place in greased 1½-qt. casserole and cover with cracker crumbs. Dot with butter. Bake for 25 minutes at 350°F. *Serves 6.*

Betty C. Rollins, The Congregational Church, Atkinson, New Hampshire

EGGPLANT ITALIANO

Cheese-filled battered eggplant rolls with a tomato-saucy flair.

FILLING:

1 cup grated mozzarella cheese	½ t. salt
½ cup grated Parmesan cheese	¼ t. pepper
⅓ cup cottage or ricotta cheese	½ t. basil or oregano
1 egg	1 T. chopped parsley

BATTER:

1 egg	⅓ cup milk
2 T. flour	1 T. cooking oil

OTHER:

2 small eggplant	flour
¼ cup cooking oil	2 6-oz. cans tomato sauce
2 T. butter	

Combine filling ingredients to make smooth paste and chill. Combine batter ingredients and beat until smooth. Peel eggplant and cut lengthwise into thin slices. Heat cooking oil and butter to 360°F. Dip eggplant slices in flour, then in batter, and sauté in hot oil until browned on both sides. Drain on paper towels. Place 2 T. chilled filling mixture on each slice and roll loosely, placing seam-side down in buttered 9"x13" baking dish. Cover with tomato sauce. Bake in oven for 15 minutes at 375°F. *Serves 8.*

Margaret Michaelsen, The Congregational Church, North Bennington, Vermont

QUICHE

Quiche, that delectable French invention, is a treat at any meal, hot or cold, can be sold at bazaars by the slice, served in bite-sized pieces as an hors d'oeuvre, or taken in a brown bag to work. Quiche can be made in a number of different ways. Here are three.

QUICHE LORRAINE

1 baked 9" pastry shell
¼ lb. bacon strips
(½ cup chopped onion)
3 eggs
1½ cups cream

½ t. salt
pinch pepper
¾ cup grated Gruyère or Swiss
    cheese
2 T. butter

Cook bacon until crisp. Drain and break up into small pieces. Scatter pieces evenly on bottom of pie shell. Sauté optional onion in bacon fat until soft, then distribute evenly in bottom of pie shell with bacon. Beat eggs, cream, salt, and pepper together. Add grated cheese. Pour egg mixture into shell on top of bacon pieces. Cut butter into tiny dots and scatter over top of custard. Set pie plate on cookie sheet and place in 375°F. oven. Bake for 40-50 minutes, checking after 25 minutes and thereafter every 10 minutes or so. Quiche is done when a silver knife inserted into center comes out clean. Cool on cake rack and serve warm. Reheats well. *Serves 6.*

SPINACH QUICHE

1 baked 9" pastry shell
¼ lb. finely diced cooked ham (½ cup)
1 10-oz. pkg. frozen chopped spinach, cooked, drained, and rechopped
2 T. chopped onion
2 T. butter

3 eggs
1½ cups heavy cream
½ t. salt
½ t. pepper
½ t. nutmeg
¼ cup grated Gruyère or Swiss cheese
1 T. butter

Scatter ham evenly over bottom of baked pie shell. Cook spinach and onion in 2 T. butter, stirring from time to time, until *all* liquid has evaporated and spinach begins to stick to pan. Remove from heat. Beat eggs with cream and seasonings. Add spinach and cheese and blend well. Pour into pastry shell. Cut the 1 T. butter into dots and sprinkle over top. Bake in 375°F. oven 40 minutes, or until set. Quiche is done when silver knife inserted into center comes out clean. Cool slightly and serve. Reheats well. *Serves 6.*

MUSHROOM QUICHE

Follow the above recipe for Spinach Quiche, substituting 1 cup cooked sliced mushrooms (drained, if you use canned) for the spinach. Cook with onion in butter until onion is golden.

CORN FLAN

Like a crustless corn quiche.

3 eggs
1 cup rich milk or half-and-half
4 T. melted butter
1 pt. frozen corn niblets, thawed
½ t. salt
¼ t. pepper

few grains cayenne pepper
¼ t. nutmeg
½ lb. Vermont cheddar cheese, thinly sliced
2 T. grated Parmesan cheese

Beat together eggs, milk, and butter. Stir in corn and seasonings. Place half of mixture in buttered pie pan or 1½-qt. baking dish. Spread with cheddar cheese, top with remaining corn mixture, and sprinkle with Parmesan cheese. Bake at 325°F. for approximately 45 minutes or until set. Let stand a few minutes before cutting. *Serves 6.*

Margaret Michaelsen, North Bennington Congregational Church, North Bennington, Vermont

FISH & SEAFOOD

MARIT'S FISH CASSEROLE

Fish and macaroni in a nutmeggy cream sauce.

1 lb. uncooked white fish fillets
1½ cups medium white sauce
½ t. salt
1½ t. nutmeg

2 eggs, separated
1 cup elbow macaroni
cheese slices
bread crumbs

SAUCE:

¼ cup melted butter
2 T. minced parsley
1 T. lemon juice

Cut fish into small pieces. Make 1½ cups favorite white sauce and to this add salt, nutmeg, and beaten egg yolks. Cook and drain macaroni. Mix fish, macaroni, and white sauce together. Fold in stiffly beaten egg whites. Pour into buttered 1½-qt. casserole and top with cheese slices and bread crumbs. Bake at 350°F. for 30 minutes. Meanwhile, combine sauce ingredients and keep warm until fish is done. Pour over casserole and serve. *Serves 6.*

Rebecca Ulrich, Concord Unitarian Church, Concord, New Hampshire

MOCK LOBSTER CASSEROLE

Marvelous way to make the relatively inexpensive haddock into something much fancier. It works!

2 lbs. haddock fillets
salt
1 cup canned (or frozen and
    thawed) cream of shrimp
    soup
1 T. lemon juice or sherry

½ t. minced onion
⅛ t. garlic powder
¼ cup melted butter
½ t. Worcestershire sauce
¾ cup bread crumbs or crushed
    Ritz crackers

Place fish in greased 2-qt. casserole. Sprinkle with salt. Mix soup with sherry or lemon juice. Pour over fish. Bake uncovered for 20 minutes at 375°F. While baking, sauté onion and garlic in butter. Remove from heat and add Worcestershire sauce. Then blend with crumbs. Sprinkle crumb mixture over fish and bake 10 minutes more. *Serves 6.*

Cheryl Tutt, Ascutney Union Church, Ascutney, Vermont

FISH CASSEROLE

Served at the Maundy Thursday Supper of Northfield's United Church, this casserole can be changed by varying the herbs used to flavor it.

1½ lbs. haddock fillets cut into
    2" strips
3 cups soft fresh bread, diced
    and pushed down in cup
    (about 7 slices)
1 medium onion, minced
pinch salt
pinch or pinches of herb or
    combination of herbs: sweet
    basil, thyme, savory,
    marjoram, rosemary

2 cans cream of mushroom soup
½ cup milk
cracker crumbs
butter

Lay half the fish on bottom of greased 9"x13" casserole. Mix bread crumbs with onion, salt, and a pinch or so of herbs. Top fish layer with half this stuffing. Mix 1 can mushroom soup with ¼ cup milk and pour over stuffing. Repeat layers, ending with second can of soup mixed with remaining ¼ cup milk. Cover with cracker crumbs and dot with butter. Bake uncovered 1 hour at 350°F. *Serves 8.*

Doris Seal, The United Church, Northfield, Vermont

FABULOUS FLOUNDER FILLETS

Absolutely fantastic!

6 large flounder fillets (about 2 lbs.)
½ t. salt

6 slices tomato
12 slices (approximately 4"x4") Gruyère or Swiss cheese

Sprinkle fillets on both sides with salt, then roll each up. In 9"x13" greased baking dish, place a flounder roll, beside it a tomato slice, and next to that a pair of cheese slices. Begin the next row with a tomato slice, then cheese, then flounder roll, and start the third row with cheese, then flounder, and then tomato. After all ingredients are used up, there should be a diagonal pattern in the way the flounder, tomato, and cheese line up. Preheat oven to 400°F.

SAUCE:

1 4-oz. can sliced mushrooms
2 medium onions, sliced
2 T. butter
1½ T. flour
1½ t. salt
¼ cup minced parsley

1 cup light cream
6 T. sherry
1½ cups uncooked long-grain rice
¾ cup snipped parsley

Drain mushrooms, reserving liquid. In 2-qt. saucepan, sauté mushrooms and onion in butter until golden. Stir in flour, salt, and parsley, then add cream, mushroom liquid combined with enough water to make ½ cup, and sherry, stirring until all is well mixed. Bring to boil. Pour over fish, tomato, and cheese. Bake 15-20 minutes, or until fillets are golden and easily flaked with fork, but still moist.

Meanwhile, cook rice. Stir snipped parsley into cooked rice. When fish is done, spoon rice along sides of dish. *Serves 6.*

Don Wyant, Woodmont Congregational Church, Milford, Connecticut

GOURMET SHRIMP

A good dish if you feel like splurging on shrimp without going to a lot of trouble.

2 lbs. shelled deveined medium
    shrimp (fresh or frozen)
3 qts. boiling water
1 t. salt
1 T. lemon juice
3 T. butter
1 cup chopped onion
1 cup chopped green pepper
1 10½-oz. can cream of
    mushroom soup

1 cup sour cream
⅓ cup catsup
1 6-oz. can sliced mushrooms,
    drained
1 t. lemon juice
¼ t. salt
⅛ t. pepper
¼ cup dry white wine

Add shrimp to 3 qts. boiling water seasoned with 1 t. salt and 1 T. lemon juice. Boil 3 minutes. Drain. Melt butter in large skillet over medium heat. Add onion and green pepper. Sauté until onion is transparent. Add soup, sour cream, catsup, mushrooms, 1 t. lemon juice, ¼ t. salt, pepper, wine, and cooked shrimp. Reduce heat, stir, and simmer gently for 5 minutes. Serve over hot rice. *Serves 8.*

Lillian Gerlander, Woodmont United Church of Christ, Milford, Connecticut

SHRIMP AND RICE CASSEROLE

The dill makes the difference.

1 cup rice, cooked and drained
½ lb. sharp cheddar cheese,
    grated
2 cups cooked shrimp
4 eggs, separated

¾ cup milk
¼ t. pepper
¼ t. onion salt
¼ t. dill weed

Mix rice, cheese, and shrimp (reserve some cheese for top). Mix egg yolks and milk and combine with shrimp mixture. Season with pepper, onion salt, and dill weed. Beat egg whites stiff and fold in. Turn into greased 2-qt. casserole. Sprinkle reserved cheese on top. Bake at 375°F. for 30 minutes. *Serves 8.*

Catherine B. Anderson, United Methodist Church of the Hamptons, Hampton, New Hampshire

MAIN DISH POTATO SALAD

This salad recipe, over 50 years old and handed down from the Bedford Men's Club (since disbanded), is now served at the Unity Club Harvest Supper every October to 450-600 people. Here, it is cut down to serve 8.

2 lbs. potatoes
3 stalks celery, chopped
1 lb. rump veal (or lean pork)
1 large onion

1 pimiento
salt and pepper to taste
whipped salad dressing
1 head lettuce

Cook peeled potatoes, cool, and dice. Mix in celery. Cook veal, cool, and dice. Grind onion and dice pimiento. Add with veal to potatoes. Salt and pepper to taste, then mix with salad dressing, and serve on a bed of lettuce. *Serves 8.*

Bedford Presbyterian Church, Bedford, New Hampshire

HOT POTATO SALAD

Made with onion and hard-boiled eggs.

6 medium potatoes
2 hard-boiled eggs, chopped
4 slices bacon, diced
¼ cup minced onion

1 egg, beaten
¼ cup cider vinegar
1¾ t. salt

Cook potatoes. Add chopped eggs. Fry bacon and onion until a delicate brown. Strain, reserving bacon fat. Add fat slowly to beaten egg and beat well. Add vinegar and salt and pour mixture over potatoes. Mix lightly to blend well; heat in double boiler. Serve hot. *Serves 6.*

Mary Kay Royer, Center Congregational Church, Torrington, Connecticut

SPAGHETTI SALAD

Essentially a "potato" salad — but with pasta!

1 8-oz. pkg. thin spaghetti
4 hard-boiled eggs
1 green pepper, cut fine
1 stalk celery, cut fine
1 t. finely grated or minced
     onion

salt and pepper to taste
½ of 5-oz. jar green olives, cut
     fine, and a few slices for top
     of salad
whipped salad dressing (*not*
     mayonnaise)

Cook spaghetti, drain, and rinse through with cold water. Drain again, add remaining ingredients, and mix thoroughly. Chill in refrigerator for a few hours before serving to allow flavors to blend. *Serves 6-8.*

Mrs. Albert G. Clark, United Church of Christ, Keene, New Hampshire